COSBY'S

LOVE CHILD

The Untold Story of Autumn Jackson the Alleged Daughter of Entertainer Bill Cosby

By:

Jewel Star

COSBY'S LOVE CHILD

The Untold Story of Autumn Jackson the Alleged Daughter of Entertainer Bill Cosby

By:

Jewel Star

Indie Book Published 2015

Jewel Star
PO Box 192
Ehrenberg AZ 85334

Books may be purchased in quantity through Createspace, or via the author's website: www.JewelStarAuthor.com

Cover Photograph:
Sunday Favor

Library of Congress Registration # 1-1954203111

@ 2014 Jewel Star, COSBY'S LOVE CHILD: The Untold Story of Autumn Jackson the alleged Daughter of Entertainer Bill Cosby

Biography & Memoir | Leaders & Notable People | Rich & Famous | Parenting &

Relationships | Conflict Management | Family Relationships | Dysfunctional Relationships

@ Jewel Star—1st Edition, Print Edition
ISBN # 978-0-692-35458-2

ACKNOWLEDGEMENTS:

Many thanks to my family and friends who had untold patience and gave undying support during the ordeal concerning my niece Autumn Jackson.

Special thanks to my niece Autumn Jackson who supported my writing a book about a difficult time in her life.

A warm thank you to Carol Linda Greener and Warren Talbot III for your perseverance in proofing my book. Your input was extremely helpful. Thank you Attorney Jesse Sam Owens for previewing my book and sharing your thoughts.

Always, I must thank my college professor, Robert Kirk Ph.D. for his belief in my writing abilities and coaxing me forever forward.

Last but not least, I would like to thank Attorney Robert Baum for providing "public record" copies I would have been hard pressed to locate. They were a tremendous help in keeping this story as accurate as possible.

ABOUT THE TITLE:

"Cosby's 'love child'" was a coined phrase that was used in news reports the year after Autumn Jackson was arrested for the attempted extortion of Bill Cosby. The use of the term "love child" was not about proof of paternity, but about a young woman who was the alleged result of a sexual affair.

Contents

Relationships | Conflict Management | Family Relationships | Dysfunctional Relationships

@ Jewel Star—1st Edition, Print Edition
ISBN # 978-0-692-35458-2

ACKNOWLEDGEMENTS:

Many thanks to my family and friends who had untold patience and gave undying support during the ordeal concerning my niece Autumn Jackson.

Special thanks to my niece Autumn Jackson who supported my writing a book about a difficult time in her life.

A warm thank you to Carol Linda Greener and Warren Talbot III for your perseverance in proofing my book. Your input was extremely helpful. Thank you Attorney Jesse Sam Owens for previewing my book and sharing your thoughts.

Always, I must thank my college professor, Robert Kirk Ph.D. for his belief in my writing abilities and coaxing me forever forward.

Last but not least, I would like to thank Attorney Robert Baum for providing "public record" copies I would have been hard pressed to locate. They were a tremendous help in keeping this story as accurate as possible.

ABOUT THE TITLE:

"Cosby's 'love child'" was a coined phrase that was used in news reports the year after Autumn Jackson was arrested for the attempted extortion of Bill Cosby. The use of the term "love child" was not about proof of paternity, but about a young woman who was the alleged result of a sexual affair.

Contents

Chapter 1

REUNION

1982

"This is my daughter, Autumn."

Shawn, my soon to be sister-in-law, spoke with a decided drawl as she introduced me to her oldest child.

"Hell-O," Autumn said as she tugged at the edges of her frilly dress. What struck me the most about the child was her winning smile. I liked her at once.

"How old are you?" I asked.

"Seven," she said and held up seven tiny fingers to show me how many.

"Autumn, do you remember your Uncle Ricky?" her mother asked.

"Uncle Ricky!" Autumn squealed, and ran to give him a big hug.

Almost as soon as Richard and I arrived, the tall, model-attractive, long-haired, Shawn Thompson said under her breath, but loud enough for me to hear, "Autumn is Bill Cosby's child."

1997

Mid-January, two devastating events concerning Bill Cosby were broadcast on the same day.

I had been doing dishes, and was half listening to a television that was on in the living room. A special news report was being broadcast and it grabbed my attention.

"Entertainer Bill Cosby's son Ennis was shot and killed last night," a news reporter stated.

I ran to the television, and with a soapy glove I turned the volume up.

"Ennis Cosby, son of entertainer Bill Cosby, pulled over to change a flat tire," the reporter continued. "An unknown assailant shot him in the head. A witness said the killer was a white man wearing a knit cap."

The same story was airing on every channel. I was stunned by the news. I thought about how I would feel if my son had been found lying on the ground.

With that unthinkable image still haunting me, my teenage son called from school, "Have you heard the news? Someone is claiming to be Bill Cosby's illegitimate child and just tried to extort him for forty-million dollars. Two people were arrested."

"Did they say who the two people were?"

"No, they didn't give any names," he replied.

"I wonder if it was Autumn?"

"Could it be anyone else?"

When I hung up with my son, I called my mother-in-law, Autumn's grandmother, Lois Maxfield. I knew she would know what was going on.

"I just heard the news. Did Shawn and Autumn get arrested?" I asked.

"It's true," Lois said. "Autumn was arrested, but not Shawn."

"Then who was the other person?"

"A 54-year-old man," Lois told me. "That's all I know."

"Oh no," I said. I knew Cosby had been supporting Autumn and helping her through school.

"I have to go," she said, and she hung up.

Autumn's name was on all the television news channels. The only picture shown was a courtroom artist's impression that didn't look like her. The eyes were too beady, and the character portrayed too sinister. That was not the Autumn I remembered.

I called Lois again.

"I just saw a report about Autumn on the news. Who's going to bail her out?" I asked.

"I don't know yet," she answered.

I knew there weren't many possibilities. Autumn's family core was small: her mother, her grandmother, and her Uncle Ricky (Richard), whom I was married to and that made me her aunt by marriage. Since Cosby was the purported father, he wasn't going to help. Paradoxically, he was the one person who could have been depended on to come to Autumn's rescue, or at least I would have assumed as much since it was apparent he was supportive of her schooling.

୧C୨୦୨

Richard and I had just settled in for the evening when the phone rang. It was Lois.

"This isn't the time to talk about it," Richard said.

"What was that about?" I asked when he hung up the phone.

"My mother wants me to bail out Autumn."

"Isn't there anyone else who could do it?" I asked, knowing there wasn't. "How much is the bail?"

"Two hundred and fifty thousand dollars."

Richard and I talked about posting Autumn's bail. We weren't even sure we could. A part of me wanted to leave her there. Another part of me, the maternal part, understood that jail wasn't a place anyone wants to be. Trials take a long time to roll around so I could understand Lois's concern.

Richard called to find out what it would take to bail her out without having to come up with the required ten percent non-refundable cash which would have been twenty-five thousand dollars.

Ultimately, we would have to turn over titles to our vehicles and titles to our property. If Autumn skipped bail, everything we owned would be stripped away. We would literally be left standing in the street scratching our heads, barefoot and homeless. I hadn't seen Autumn in several years and didn't know the person she had become as an adult. I was leery of putting up everything we had worked hard for over the course of eighteen years. What if she was capable of running?

Lois kept calling, and was crying harder every time she called. Richard just wanted her to stop. He made the final decision that we would risk everything in order to stop Autumn's grandmother's tears.

❦

It took two days to collect and send the documents required by the government to secure Autumn's bail. After that, Richard and his mother drove two hours to the federal building in Sacramento, California to sign papers for Autumn's release. She had been arrested in New York City, New York, by the FBI (Federal Bureau of Investigation), which made her case federal. She would be allowed to stay with her grandmother, but she would have to return to New York for her court dates.

Richard and his mother were gone all night. They had to wait at the airport for Autumn to come in on a red-eye special.

It was five-o'clock in the morning when they drove up the dirt road leading to our home. As soon as Autumn stepped from the car, I could see she still had the same sparkling smile. She was not the monster the press had made her out to be.

"Good morning Autumn," I said, while clutching my robe around my neck against the frosty morning air.

"Hell-O," Autumn said making separate words of the syllables the way she had done as a child.

She walked in my direction, wearing a road-weary grin.

We hugged.

"I'll call you tomorrow after you have had a chance to get some rest," I told her.

"Okay," she said, sleepy eyed.

She was only out of the car briefly before getting back in. Richard drove them the twenty minutes further it would take to arrive at her grandmother's house on the other side of the lake we lived near.

$$\text{《℃ↄ》}$$

"I'm beat," Richard said when he returned. "I'm going to bed. Take messages."

We went inside and closed the door. All was quiet for a while. A calm before the storm, as it turned out.

About mid-morning, I looked out the window and saw a van pulling up. Someone knocked at the door. "Who is it?" I asked.

"I'm looking for directions," a woman yelled back.

I opened the door to a short woman with hair that was new-wave red. "Is this where Richard Jesperson lives?" she asked. A man stood behind her balancing a camera that was gazing at me with one large eye.

"I don't have any comment to make," I told them.

"We're just going to wait out here," the woman said. And wait they did—for two days!

Richard and I had spent many years in Lake County, California, high above the wine country, with hardly a phone call or a visitor, but now the phone was ringing off the hook. When he signed for Autumn's bail the information, including our address and phone number, became public record.

People Magazine called first. We even received a call from a press agent in London. Calls from reporters were peppered with calls from friends and relatives who shared our disbelief about what had happened.

"Is she really Cosby's daughter?" everyone asked.

"Do I believe she is?" I had to ask myself.

One reporter asked what color Shawn was. I held my "no comment" ground, but I knew it would come out soon enough that Shawn was not the same color as Bill.

From outside, it looked as if there were a party going on. Parked in our yard were a score of cars and vans topped with antennas, satellites, and scanners. Cameras were propped and ready for any movement coming from inside the house.

A couple of retired neighbors were upset when vehicles started parking on their property as well. "Do you know what's going on?" one of them asked. They had tried to run off the annoying intruders.

"Our niece is in some trouble, and we bailed her out," I told them, leaving it at that. If they ever figured out who our niece was they never mentioned it.

On the second day of the encampment, Richard snuck out to keep an eye on things from afar.

I had already missed a college class because of the press sentries watching the house, and I didn't want to miss another. I decided to take my chances and run for the car. Before I could get the door opened the reporters from the television program *Inside Edition* had me cornered.

"Are you Autumn's aunt?" an easy-speaking Tony Cox asked holding a microphone poised toward my face.

"Yes," I answered, trying to be polite.

He asked me some other questions that were easy enough, but then he asked a hard one. "Is she (Autumn) capable of trying to extort money from this . . . celebrity (Bill Cosby)?"

"I knew Autumn as a little girl, and as my niece. And I love her very much. I know she's a wonderful person at heart. I don't know what brought all this up or what happened," I said in her defense.

"Is Autumn staying with you?" he asked.

I was flustered at the reporter's boldness. I jumped into my car and drove away.

Later that same day, I saw the impromptu interview being shown on national television. I sat on the couch and watched myself answering Mr. Cox's questions.

The same program reported that Autumn had an active warrant for writing bad checks in Florida. Richard and I hadn't heard anything about that. We could only wonder how little we knew about our niece.

§c)⌒ɔ₎

I was home alone and the media circus outside our door was becoming out of control. One reporter claiming to be with *The National Enquirer* called on his cell phone. "Just wave through the window if you want to talk," he said to the answering machine.

When I didn't pick up, he started rapping on our mobile home's single-pane windows.

A constant line of reporters were knocking on the front and back doors throughout the day. Though I had been fighting the idea it was time to leave.

Richard slipped in the back door when it was well after dark. He gathered up my travel bags and headed out the door. "Let's go!" he demanded.

It was so dark out I was walking blindly—tripping over sticks and small bushy plants. "Get down!" Richard whispered rather loudly.

I looked beside me, and I was barely able to make out my husband's shadowy figure. His 6 foot 2 inch body was hunched down close to the ground.

Suddenly, I felt ten again. We were dressed all in black, playing a game of hide and seek while crawling through poison oak and other scratchy brush, though in reality this was no game.

It was definitely a wintry night with the temperature dropping to the low twenties. The camped-out reporters were sitting in their cars to keep warm. They couldn't see us from where they were parked. We made it to the edge of a cliff and had to slide down a muddy bank. There was a frigidly cold creek at the bottom we had to be careful not to fall into. "Get down!" Richard hissed as we approached the road and car beams shined on us. He was playing the charade with militant seriousness.

He took me by boat across Clear Lake to Lois's house where Autumn was staying. When Richard and I walked in all dressed up like Ninja warriors Autumn started to laugh. Her laughter was infectious, and she soon had us laughing too.

"Look at you," she said, as a smile lit up her small face.

"We're smarter than the cameramen," Richard said, getting serious again. He wanted to watch both houses from a distance, so he would be staying in the town of Clearlake with a friend.

Before heading back to the boat he said, "Lock yourselves in."

As soon as I sat down the phone rang. It continued to ring every few minutes. If it wasn't the press, it was Autumn's mother, Shawn, or her boyfriend, Tony, whom we would be meeting in the near future.

Chapter 2

CHOCOLATE CHIPS

Autumn looked the same as when she was a teenager. She was petite, and at her ideal weight after a week of not eating much in jail. It was her small hands that fascinated me most. She had perfectly shaped fingers with nail tips that grew out opaque white against her dark skin. She talked with her hands, using them to express herself. They danced before her, emphasizing the important points.

"Are you going to have a trial?" I started, eager to hear the details of what had happened.

"Yes," she answered.

"What was it like in jail?"

"You have to strip down, squat down, and then cough. I mean really cough!" She coughed out loud to show me what she meant. "I didn't get to be with everyone else," she continued. "I was at first, but then they put me in a room by myself. I didn't like that." Her naturally straight hair had been dyed black from its normal dark brown, and she was wearing it short. It was shiny from washing, and thick locks jostled on top of her head when she talked.

I asked her about the 54-year-old man she was arrested with. "Who is Jose Medina?"

"He goes by Yosie," she said. "We were working on a children's show called *Down on the Farm with Chocolate Chips and the Prairie Dogs*." The name was as cumbersome as the storyline that went with it.

"What does a children's show about chocolate chips and dogs have to do with Bill Cosby?" I asked.

"That's how I got connected up with Yosie," Autumn explained. "Yosie was a guest at the Holiday Inn in Los Angeles where I was working. He told me he was a producer, and then told me about his idea for *Down on the Farm*."

Autumn's awkward tale became muddled in its telling. Then she started at the point where she had left the school in Florida. A school Cosby had enrolled her in.

"My sisters and brother called me up. They said they were

hungry and dirty, and tired of living in crack houses with our mother. They needed my help. I had to go to California and get them. I had to sell the car that Mr. Cosby bought me." Autumn said. "It was too small. I left for Los Angeles with the intention of bringing them back to Florida. To do that I had to have a bigger car so that's what I bought with the money from the one I sold."

Autumn told me that when she arrived at her mother's house things didn't go quite like she had planned. Neglected though they may be, her mother wasn't going to let Autumn take her siblings anywhere. She dropped out of school, and found a job. If she couldn't uproot the children she was going to stay close by. However, Autumn missed her, on again off again, boyfriend, Antonay (Tony) Williams, and soon wanted to return to Florida to be with him.

Autumn's story spun on. "My mother suggested that Tony come to California instead of me going back to Florida. Tony wants to be an actor. When I introduced him to Yosie, who claimed to be an important producer, Tony was very excited. Yosie put him to work as a screenwriter for the children's show."

Two other men were involved in the production as well: Boris Sabas who was from Russia, and Sid Macaraeg who was from the Philippines.

Autumn explained, "Yosie wasn't going to pay anyone until the show sold. Once it sold, Tony was going to get a percentage. Tony and my mother weren't getting along so she kicked us out of the house, and I lost my job at the Holiday Inn. I ended up going to work for Yosie, too. He said I could share Tony's percentage."

"How did you lose your job?" I asked.

"Three-hundred dollars was missing from my cash can. I went into work and my cash drawer was empty. Normally I wore the key around my neck but I couldn't find it. It was really bad timing. When my mother asked us to leave we had to move into my car and we became homeless."

"Where did you park," I asked.

"I parked at the hotel where I'd been working. Yosie wouldn't let us stay in his room. He said it was 'Kosher' and had been blessed by a rabbi, and that no one else could stay there."

"Autumn, I have to ask you something."

"What?"

"Why did you ask Bill Cosby for forty-million dollars?"

"Yosie was the one who decided how much to ask for. He told me that Mr. Cosby owed me back child support, and that I should be reimbursed at a percentage of what Mr. Cosby was worth. I thought Yosie was trying to help me. He had been a good friend up to this point, and I thought he was being supportive because he really liked me. He sounded honestly concerned that we didn't have a place to live and thought it was terrible that someone who was supposed to be my father would let me live in my car while he lived in mansions. He said he would do whatever he could to set things right and he had me write lists of things that he thought we should do so that we could remedy our situation. Yosie had Tony do research to find out how much money Mr. Cosby had. Tony and I went to the library and looked up Cosby's sponsors. Yosie called the *Globe* tabloid and checked to see what they would pay for my story. Yosie convinced me there was no way in the world a child of Bill Cosby's should be sleeping in her car." Autumn said.

"Why did you ask for the money right when Bill's son had just been killed?"

"This whole thing started way before that," Autumn said. "It was November, I think. I hadn't heard about Ennis's death until after arrangements had been made to pick up the money. My mother never told me about Mr. Cosby's other children. I had a brother no one ever told me about," she said visibly distressed, and her eyes grew liquid. "I never even got a chance to meet Ennis."

Autumn's love for her brother Aaron, and her much younger sisters Alisha and Alaina gave direction to her life. She expressed a loss for Ennis as real as if she had known him as a sibling.

§C√D§

Mary Jo White, U.S. Attorney for the Southern District of New York, prepared a statement announcing there was no evidence that the extortion attempt was related to Ennis's murder.

Still, it was impossible to dismiss the possibility of a connection, especially when Autumn told me she thought Yosie capable of such tactics.

"Tony and I didn't have anything to do with the murder," Autumn said convincingly. But she felt that Yosie was powerful enough to do something like that if he had wanted to. However, she didn't have any proof.

"The night before Ennis was killed, Yosie said that there was a person sitting in a restaurant, and that someone was going to be taken care of by the morning. Tony and I didn't know what that meant, but that was the first thing we thought of when we heard the news about Ennis."

The phone was still ringing off the hook. We were interrupted every fifteen to twenty minutes. Autumn's mother Shawn called in between the reporters.

"I don't want to talk to my mother," Autumn said as she reached for the phone. It was her mother and she talked to her. She felt her mother partially responsible even though Shawn didn't know about the rouse until just before Autumn was arrested.

When she hung up she said, "If my mother hadn't kicked us out, maybe this never would have happened."

"Why do they have a warrant out for your arrest in Florida?" I asked.

"I was homeless," she stated again. "I had to eat. I just bought food. My checking account was messed up."

"How about some tea?" I asked. We both needed to use the bathroom and take a stretch.

I stood by a large plate-glass window that overlooked the lake behind the house. The dark water lapped at the dock and I watched as slate-blue currents drifted by in slow motion. I tried to sort out all I had been told.

When our tea was ready we settled back onto overstuffed furniture in the cozy second-story living room with knotty-pine paneling.

"I don't do well with surprises," I said. "Is there anything else I should know?"

"No, there's nothing else."

We went on to talk about her life with her mother, Shawn.

"Sometimes, we had to roll up our pennies to buy milk," Autumn said. "I raised them." Autumn beamed, as if her siblings were her own children.

The subject changed to her boyfriend Tony, whom I had never met. Richard had met him only briefly a couple of years before.

"No one knows this yet, but Tony and I are engaged," Autumn confided, and a smile turned up the corners of her mouth. "He's on his way here right now," she added. "He might stay here until the trial."

Lois came home from work, and Autumn followed her into the

bedroom to talk. I went into the kitchen, sat at a round dining table, and called Richard. While the phone was ringing, I looked out at the lake to watch the glistering lights across the shore. The scene looked too peaceful in contrast to the chaos that Autumn had brought into our lives.

I filled Richard in. "Did you know Autumn's boyfriend was on his way here?"

"No, I didn't."

We hung up.

In a few minutes Richard called back and asked to talk to Autumn. She took the call. When she hung up, she came running out into the living room sobbing. "Richard doesn't want Tony to come here, but he has to!"

I waited to hear more before responding.

Autumn paced the floor in quick and worried steps. She was wearing an oversized crisp white tee shirt and black leggings. The tee shirt twisted with her movement, and the leggings form fit her flexing leg muscles. Her feet were bare and soundless on the carpet.

She was crying her heart out to the point of hysteria. It made me remember what it was like to have the kind of love that can't tolerate separation. I searched for something to say, but I could only watch her agony.

She repeated over and over again, "Tony has to be allowed to come! He's the only normalcy I have left in my life!" She waved her arms and hands like wands in front of her in an effort to make her words appear as large as she was feeling them.

Lois left for a meeting, and I talked to Autumn until she calmed down. "This is a fearful situation for all of us," I explained. "Everything is happening very fast. Just give Uncle Ricky some time to think things over." I said, trying to give her the support she needed.

"He'll just say no," she sobbed, her tears still flowing.

Autumn hadn't spent enough time with her uncle to make that kind of a judgment call. She was speaking from her own fears and insecurities.

"How did you meet Tony?" I asked.

"I was nineteen and going to school in Tallahassee," she said choking down a final sob.

Cosby had selected the school she was attending, and was fully

supporting her while she was there.

"Tony asked me to a party. He followed me around with his hands in the back pockets of my jeans. We ended up spending three days together."

Autumn told me they had been together pretty much ever since. He took her virginity, and he was the one she was going to spend the rest of her life with—she was sure of it.

"Tony would never cheat on me," Autumn shared. "Even if I have to go to prison, he would wait for me."

Autumn told me she hadn't seen Tony since she had been arrested. He had turned himself in to "help her," and now he was in trouble, too.

"We were already thinking about getting married before this happened," she said. "We found a house that's perfect for raising our family."

Autumn's childlike presence was giving way to the woman in her, a woman who was in love. She would gladly pay the punishment due as long as Tony could be by her side. Her love was desperate, maybe obsessive, and definitely romantic.

Autumn showed me pictures of Tony from his modeling school.

"He's very handsome," I told her.

Her eyes were shining, lit up with the glow of love.

Chapter 3

SNAKE MEDICINE

Reverently, I presented a silk purse to Autumn that was holding an oversized deck of cards. I had brought the oracle as a means of getting to know who Autumn had become. "Have you ever heard of the Medicine Cards?" I asked.

"I've heard about Tarot cards, and I'm curious about them." Autumn answered.

"I have a deck of Tarot cards at home if you want to try them sometime," I told Autumn. "The Medicine Cards are the latest craze, and they're fun, too. Teachers from the Native American Wolf Clan created the cards to aid in personal growth. Each animal is assigned a medicinal power dealing with a life lesson."

"I'm afraid Grandma wouldn't like this," Autumn said about our playing with the cards.

It would be our first secret.

"Look at all the cards," I instructed. "Then, shuffle them."

She shuffled the cards decorated with pictures of animals, birds, fish, and insects.

"The *Nine Totem Animals* reading is one that is done only once. It will show you the animals that will imitate your abilities and challenges. They will walk with you your whole life. Fan the cards upside-down in an arch." I told her.

She drew the cards that would be her lifelong totem. "I'm very loyal," she said when she turned up the *Dog* card that stood for loyalty.

"It's your turn to read," I told her when she picked the *Ant* card. I handed her the book that contained the definition of the cards.

She read that Ant stood for patience and that she needed to have faith in a current situation.

"Your uncle has *Ant* medicine," I shared. "Maybe you inherited your patience from him."

"Oh no!" she exclaimed when she turned up *Skunk*. "What does that mean? Do I smell or something?" She jokingly sniffed at her armpits.

We both started to laugh. Even though the situation was dire we were rekindling our friendship that had grown during her teenage years.

"You'd be surprised at the meanings for some of the cards," I told her. "*Skunk* stands for reputation, and his reputation certainly precedes him. Everyone had respect for a skunk."

"That's for sure!" Autumn agreed.

Next she picked *Butterfly* for transformation.

"I like this card better," she said.

"You'll be transformed before this whole ordeal is over," I said, teasing her with honesty, and making light of all that was too intense.

We both sucked in our breath when she turned up *Snake*.

"The book says that Snake medicine people are rare," I told her. "Since you chose this card there is a need for you to change some thought or action. It's about transmutation, like a snake shedding its skin. A sort of starting over I would think."

Autumn was able to use the cards as a distraction. Her burst of tears, now spent, left her calm and receptive. She was ready for any answers that would ease her pain—add to her understanding.

The reading was over. I scooped up the cards, and returned them to their special case.

"The cards give you a lot to think about," Autumn said.

"Yes, they do. It's been a long day. I'm going to bed and leave you to your thoughts. I'll see you in the morning." I leaned over and gave her a goodnight hug.

"Goodnight," she said, already drifting off in contemplation.

❧

In the morning, Lois made us pancakes. It always seemed so out of place to see her cooking. It was unusual that she would, as there was seldom any food in the house. Having been a waitress for many years, she usually ate at work, and even though she wasn't a waitress anymore the cupboards were always bare.

"The pancakes are delicious!" I told Lois. We all needed some comfort food.

"I never eat breakfast," Autumn said when she was offered a pancake.

"Your grandmother is cooking," I teased, "You have to eat at least one."

She didn't argue. She sat at the table, and Lois put a pancake filled plate in front of her. When Lois leaned over Autumn to hand her the syrup, she spotted a reporter climbing a fence by the boat dock at the back of the house. He was balancing his heavy camera on his shoulder. "I'll go down and tell him he's trespassing," she said.

After chasing away the reporter, Lois went out to the mailbox and retrieved a large parcel that had been sent to her from the *Globe* tabloid.

"Oh, look," she said like a delighted child. She unpacked assorted coffee, lemon, and chocolate mini-gourmet cakes out of the brown paper box. A letter sent with the package was asking her to tell her side of the story. Money was offered.

Richard had been very clear with his feelings about any of us making money from the unfortunate event, at least until after Autumn's trial. We all complied except for Autumn's mother, Shawn.

Until everything was sorted out, all funds from Cosby were stopped. Shawn had bills to pay and children to feed. Cosby had previously set up a generous trust account for Shawn which was her only income. To have it stop suddenly was a hardship.

"You know how Richard feels about us saying anything," I reminded Lois.

"My mother is saying enough for everyone," Autumn added.

Even though we were stuffed from the pancakes we decided to sample one of the small "bribery" cakes. We weren't going to send them back, nor would we be expected to. The box and the letter were then packed back up, and we each went off in different directions.

Not long after breakfast, Richard stopped by.

"I just chased off a couple of reporters with telescopic cameras. You'd better hang some sheets over the windows," he told us.

"I'll get some sheets," Lois said. She was always ready to offer help, whatever the situation.

"Now we've lost our view of the lake," I said as if it was necessary to state a known fact. It wouldn't change the fact that the curtains were going to be hung.

"I'll help hang them," Autumn offered. She didn't mind being closed in, and like her grandmother, she never hesitated at jumping in to help.

Since we didn't know if the FBI was tapping the phones, or if the reporters were listening in with their highly efficient sound equipment, we decided it might be best to have code names. Lois becomes Lo Lo.

Not very creative, I know.

"You can call me Pocahontas," Autumn suggested. "That's what they called me in jail. They said I looked like her."

"That's a mouthful, how about Pokey for short?" I suggested.

I was to be JJ which were my initials at that time.

Richard was to be called, *Rambo*, after his Rambo Rick maneuvers to slither me past the press and deliver me via a dark, cold, and watery ride to his mother's house. He watched out for us from afar and kept the reporters guessing as to our whereabouts. For the few who figured out our coordinates, he would jump out of the bushes looking like a madman and most likely scared the sweet Bejesus out of them.

Later in the day, Autumn was in high spirits. Tony would be arriving soon. Not only had Richard agreed to let Tony come after all; he had offered to pick him up from the bus station. I was quick to realize he was easily turned to putty when the women in his life turned on their tears.

We heard a car door slam at the neighbors, followed by footsteps approaching Lois's front door. A peek out the window confirmed it was Richard and Tony. The plan was to drop off Tony, and pick me up, sneaking me back home again.

A huge grin lit up Tony's face at the sight of Autumn. He walked right to her, but gave her an almost shy greeting.

"Hello," he said.

"Hell-O," Autumn said, with eyes just for him.

He was over six feet tall, and he dwarfed her small frame when he gave her a quick hug. They anxiously watched as I collected my things. They were eager to be alone. They needed to touch, to talk, and feel some relief after the arrest and all its implications.

۶ೌᢍ᠐ᦔ

Unexpectedly, the next day I missed Autumn. We had spent three days together because of the tragedy. We had shared memories, experiences, stories, tears, and thank goodness, even a few laughs. What the media had missed in all of this was Autumn's humanness. She was a palette of youth, emotion, and inexperience.

Every television program and news report that spoke of Autumn also included the latest information on the death of Bill's son, Ennis Cosby.

After Ennis's death, a horde of press converged where his body was found. The car had yet to be towed, and the emergency lights were ominously still flashing.

The police were calling it a random act of violence, or perhaps something racial, but there was still the possibility that he had been followed. If it was a robbery attempt, nothing had been taken. There were no signs of a struggle.

Cosby's publicist, David Brokaw, said, "Everyone feels like they lost a son."

Autumn felt as if she had lost a brother, albeit one she never knew existed.

Even though reporters always confirmed that there didn't appear to be a connection between the murder and the extortion, the timing was eerily chilling. One story was not told without mention of the other. So in that way, Autumn and Ennis would always be connected.

In an effort to help Autumn, Richard set up a conference call so that Tony could talk to Autumn's lawyer.

At the appointed time, Richard and Tony each picked up an extension of the phone and talked to Autumn's appointed legal counsel. Robert Balm's eastern accent represented another world; one that was quite removed from our small country town.

Richard spent over an hour listening to Tony tell Baum his side of the story. They talked about what he might say should he be called to give testimony.

When Richard told me Tony all but accused Yosie of murder, my greatest fears surfaced.

I read to Richard from an article that came out on Jose (Yosie) Medina. He had been charged with loan brokering and theft by deception in 1990.

The next day I called Autumn and asked her if she knew Yosie was on parole for a previous charge.

"No, not until I heard it on the news," she said.

"Are you sure you don't know anything about the murder?" I pressed.

"No, but Yosie told us that Cosby might have had Ennis murdered because he had found out about me. After hearing the reports about Ennis, we saw a strange car in the parking lot below Yosie's room. Yosie said Cosby had sent an assassin after me, because I was about to tell my story. I was scared for my life."

"Why do you think Bill would have his own son murdered?"

"I remember hearing things when I was growing up, and how Mr. Cosby was not the saint everyone thought he was. He was mixed up with drugs and gangsters right along—even other women. He's a very powerful man, and I don't know what he might try to do. Yosie told us there were hit-men in the car below just waiting for me to come outside. When I tried to leave the room Yosie stopped me. A man knocked on the door, and we all freaked out. He said he was from room service, but we knew he wasn't. We wouldn't open the door."

When I told Richard about the car Autumn saw, he said he had been watching a strange car in our neighborhood that was the same type as a mob person might drive.

Richard said, "A forty-million dollar deal gone bad could have some repercussions."

We had no idea what Yosie was like. What Autumn had told me about him hadn't been good. We had no idea just how angry this Yosie guy might be, or what he might try to do. He was still in jail, unable to secure a bond, and he might be really upset about being there.

"Autumn and Tony could be in danger," Richard said. He told them to keep their eyes open.

Equally as bad, he explained we could become targets ourselves since the media had led everyone to believe that Autumn was staying with us. We went outside and searched around and under the house for bombs.

I called Autumn every day to see how she was doing and ask her questions that had come up in the news. During one such phone call I asked her, "Did Cosby's wife know about you before this happened?"

"I don't know," she said. "I thought she did."

"I sure hope she did," I told Autumn. I couldn't imagine what Cosby's wife must have been going through. Camille had lost her son, and in such a loathsome way. That had to be painful enough. Now her husband was being publicly disgraced, and all in a matter of days.

I couldn't help but wonder what Bill and Camille's four daughters were thinking about all of this as well. How confusing to have just lost a brother, only to find out you may have a long-lost sister. Their hearts must have been equally torn.

Cosby told Dan Rather during an interview that he had always imagined that if one of his children was to get hurt he would go and get multiple .357 magnums. Then, in nearly the next breath, he was confessing to a sexual indiscretion that he called "the rendezvous."

At first he denied that Autumn was his daughter, but he didn't deny that he had made love to Shawn. He went on to say he had known that Autumn was not his, because it wasn't his name on her birth certificate. He even announced that he had a copy of Autumn's birth certificate.

"Why would Cosby have Autumn's birth certificate?" I asked Richard.

After Rather's original interview with Cosby failed to air in full, CBS released a transcript where Cosby sang a new tune about Autumn being his, saying, "There's a possibility."

Baum, Autumn's attorney, told the press that Cosby's acknowledgment of the affair was a "substantial change from critical comments that came from Cosby's representatives earlier."

If the whole thing was not already a soap opera, it certainly was when a California truck driver, Jerald Jackson, came forward and claimed it was his name on Autumn's birth certificate, and that he was Autumn's dad.

"Bill is paying him to say those things," Shawn said the next time she called.

I read Richard the article that had come out in a tabloid where Jerald had made his confession.

"I would love to get my hands around Jerald's neck," Richard said, remembering old vendettas.

As it turned out, when Autumn was a baby, Richard had rescued her and Shawn from the gun-toting Jackson, who was supposedly arrested for having a sawed-off shotgun.

Chapter 4

DINNER PARTIES

"Look at all the stars," Richard said. They were silvery in the dark winter sky. "Seeing the stars is one of the greatest things about living in the country."

"I love living in the country." Tony said. "Someday I would like to have a place like yours."

"Me too," Autumn agreed.

"I didn't know you liked living in the country," I said to Autumn, always having thought of her as a city girl.

"Oh yeah," she said. "I like getting up and looking out at the lake at Grandma's."

Tony lit a vanilla-essence cigar, took a puff and handed it to Autumn.

Earlier that evening, Richard had taken us all out to dinner.

"I'll have the Alaskan king crab," Tony said, ordering the most expensive item on the menu. As an afterthought he added. "Fish is so expensive in California. In Florida we get big tubs and fill 'em with all kinds of shellfish for a little bit of nothin'. We build a fire underneath and cook the stew outside."

"Staying on the lake will be perfect if you like to fish," I said.

"I miss fishing," Tony said. "It's hard to look out at the lake and not be able to drop a line."

"I'll buy you a license," Richard promised. "I have a fishing pole you can use."

Autumn had come straight from jail with nothing but the clothes on her back. Fortunately, she fit into her grandmother's clothing. However, selecting from the closet of a seventy-year-old was not going to be easy. Autumn's mother, Shawn who was still living in southern California, had been asked to send clothes and/or money, but neither had arrived.

Tony had shown up with a military footlocker full of clothes and a few dollar bills in his pocket.

"This is for you," I told Autumn as I handed her a brocade jewelry pouch across the dinner table. Inside were four pairs of earrings.

"Did you make these?" she asked, her face lighting up at the gift.

"Yes, I thought you could use some earrings, I haven't seen you wearing any. I always feel better when I have some jewelry on."

"Look, Tony," she said showing him her new treasures. She included him in everything.

I tried to see what Autumn saw in Tony. Was it his angular face and large eyes, or was it the suave air he had about himself? He did seem very sincere where Autumn was concerned.

Unlike Autumn's naturally straight hair, his was extremely kinky and close cut to his head.

"Thank goodness, he doesn't wear his ball-cap backwards." Richard had mentioned to me earlier.

"I love this woman," Tony said convincingly when he looked over at Autumn.

I had already seen that love-struck look in Autumn's eyes when she looked at him.

Other than her obvious delight over the gift of the earrings, Autumn was unusually quiet during dinner. There had been many times when I had trouble keeping up with her in a one-on-one conversation. While we had been together at her grandmother's she told me, "I'm a little shy and on the quiet side."

I found Autumn's self-image surprising. She had never been shy and quiet with me. As a teenager she had been vivacious and very verbal about what she thought. I remember one summer when she was up visiting her grandmother, she came over to swim in our pool with my children which were her cousins by marriage. She stopped to have a chat with me while I cut up some watermelon in the kitchen.

"I'm going to be rich, very rich," she ruminated. "I'm going to design big beautiful buildings and have as much money as Mr. Cosby."

I had left her to her pipe dreams, not letting on that it would be pretty tough to make as much money as Cosby under any normal circumstances. It was old news that he was most likely one of the richest performers in the entertainment industry.

One afternoon, during the next week, Autumn and Tony stopped by. I had only heard bits and pieces of Tony's side of the story. I offered them some homemade strawberry liqueur. The soothing liquid helped to relax everyone's tongues. Tony didn't waste any time letting me know that Yosie was the mastermind behind the extortion. "Yosie was behind this whole thing," he said, leaning forward on the couch.

Autumn grimaced at the mention of Yosie's name.

"This is big!" Tony exclaimed. "This is really big! Yosie has a lot of money and power. He always had a lot of money around. He showed me a briefcase that was stuffed with five hundred thousand dollars! One time Yosie got mad at the kids who were doing the acting in the children's show, and he threw three thousand dollars on the floor in front of them, and said, 'Here, this is what you're here for!'"

"Did the children ever get paid?" I asked.

"I don't know," Tony answered.

Though Tony thought a lot of Yosie's dealings were legal, he also thought Yosie might be laundering money.

"He has bank accounts from all over the world logged onto his computer," Tony said. "And they have a lot of money in them. He even traded in gems and jewels."

"If he had so much money, why wasn't he paying you to work for him?" I asked.

"We were going to get paid a percentage when the show sold."

I was going to ask him how he felt about sharing his percentage with Autumn but I left it alone.

"When this all comes out, you'll see how big this is," Tony continued. "Yosie has a phone book with all these important names in it. He even has Hillary's personal phone number."

"Hillary Clinton's phone number?" I asked.

"Yes, and a lot of other big names as well."

Autumn and Tony assumed he had Cosby's phone number too.

"Yosie told us he called Cosby and told him to send Autumn some money," Tony went on.

"Were you there when he called Bill?" I asked.

"No, he told us he called him in the middle of the night."

"That would have been the right time," Autumn said. "Mr. Cosby often called my mom in the middle of the night."

The next day Autumn received two hundred dollars, supposedly from Cosby.

"Yosie really got upset after Autumn told him how much she had received," Tony said. "Yosie shouted, 'That was not the deal!' He kicked the air, and said, 'This is war!'"

"Yosie got upset about a lot of things," Autumn said. "He'd have those kind of outbursts quite often."

"What did he do when he got upset?" I asked. "Did he throw things?"

"He would kick and punch the air. He didn't throw things, or anything like that," Autumn said.

"Did you know that Yosie had a record for fraud?" I asked, directing my question to Tony.

"No, we didn't know anything about that." Tony answered.

"Do you think he could have had something to do with Ennis's murder?" I pressed.

Tony repeated what Autumn had told me about Yosie making an off-color remark the night before the murder.

"I don't know about anything that would indicate that Yosie was involved, but one time, I overheard him talking to some men, and he threatened their families if they didn't do what he told them to do." Tony explained.

"Why didn't you pull out?" I asked.

"I felt like a pawn in Yosie's game," Tony answered.

Tony had stayed behind when Autumn and Yosie left to pick up the money they were told Cosby was going to give her in reaction to her request. When they were arrested, Tony caught a plane to New York. He tried to see Autumn, which he wasn't able to do, and then he turned himself in to the FBI.

"I wanted to help Autumn," Tony said. "The FBI told me the best way to help her was by pleading guilty. I talked to them for thirty-two hours, and told them the truth about everything."

His pleading guilty made him the prosecution's witness against Autumn. In answer to that Tony said, "They tricked me. I told the FBI that Autumn and I need to be put in the Witness Protection Program."

"Why is that?" I asked.

"Yosie might come after us," he said.

"He's still in jail."

"Believe me, if he wants to get to us, he has the connections."

"Do you think he would try to have you killed?" I asked, remembering our recent bomb search.

"We don't know what he might do," Tony said.

"That's very scary," I responded. "Are they going to put you in the program?"

"We don't know yet."

The liqueur glasses were empty.

"Would you like a refill?" I asked. Not waiting for an answer I poured more of the strawberry-red liquid. The sun was shining brightly in a vivid blue sky, even though it was February. It was nice enough to have the front door open for a bit. Autumn was not acclimatized to the Northern California weather, and she seldom took her coat off when she came to visit. I asked Autumn, "Are you warm enough with the door open?"

She pulled her coat closer around her, and answered, "I'm fine for now."

A cool breeze rolled off the sugar pines and rustled the barren oaks. We breathed in the fresh air to cleanse ourselves of thoughts about extortion and murder.

I turned to Autumn and asked, "Do you really believe that Bill Cosby is your father?" It seemed like a funny thing to be asking her, because I knew she believed it as a child. But I wanted to know how she felt as an adult.

"He is my father," she said calmly and with conviction. She had never questioned otherwise.

"Will Bill take a blood test?"

"I already asked him to when I was seventeen. He was going to. It was even set up with his doctor, but then he said it might leak out that he was taking the test, and that wouldn't be good for him. When this all happened, my lawyer sent a letter asking him to take the test, but so far he has refused."

"It would be better for you to be Bill's child," I said, thinking of the imminent trial.

♔

Our foursome dinner-parties became a weekend ritual. It gave Autumn and Tony a break from living with Lois, and it gave Richard and me a chance to stay connected to all that was going on.

The next time they came over, Richard had a bubbling Shrimp Creole going on the stove.

"Autumn, come and help me with the drinks," I requested.

The men went outside, and left us to chitchat. "Have you talked to your mother?" I asked.

"Oh, yeah, she's having a lot of trouble with the press."

Autumn's first court date in New York was coming up and it had been decided that I would be going as her chaperone. "What does your mother think about me going to New York with you?"

"She thinks she should be going instead of you, but I don't want to go with her."

"You don't have to," I reassured her.

The only other option was for Autumn to go by herself. The government would provide a room for her at the YWCA.

"I'm glad I get to go with you so you don't have to stay at the YWCA. I don't think it would be safe enough. Who knows what someone with a warped sense of dedication to Cosby might try to do. The last thing you need is a stalker."

"That's for sure," Autumn agreed.

The smell of the fish stew, and the browning garlic bread brought the guys back in.

After dishing up dinner, Richard asked Autumn, "Are you okay about going to New York with Jewel?"

"Yes, but my mother isn't going to like it. She'll probably call you and tell you she should be going."

"When pigs fly," Richard said, coming out with one of his many farm-boy sayings. "She doesn't have a say in this."

Autumn lit up at the expression Richard used, and exclaimed, "You're all country, Uncle Ricky!"

The dinner was delicious, but it made Tony homesick for big pots of boiled shellfish cooking over an open fire.

Jumping in as mates often do, Autumn would accent Tony's stories with her memories of when they had lived together in Florida. "Justice was the name of our dog," Autumn said.

"Justice was my dog first," Tony said correcting her.

"That's right," she said. "He was Tony's dog first."

I was starting to understand why she held her tongue around him. It wasn't about being shy. Being in love can lead one into making a lot of concessions. All that Autumn knew was how Tony touched her soul. And to her, that was all that mattered. "Tony is the only one I can trust," she had told me earlier.

I had responded to Autumn by saying, "But he turned State's evidence against you."

"He was trying to help me." She was very loyal to the man who was twenty six—four years older than she was.

There was no point in arguing it further.

After being served a second helping of fish soup, Tony told stories about growing up in the country. "I fished every day," he said.

"Did you ever see any alligators?" I asked.

"Sure, there were plenty of 'gators, but I didn't hang around when I saw one. Some of my friends would mess with 'em, though.

When Tony finished his stories about the days of camping and fishing, he drifted into a moment of deep thought. "I wish I had never come to California," he said out loud.

As much as Autumn tried to forget her predicament, and we made an effort to avoid the topic, everything revolved around it and eventually came back to it as if it were a giant magnet.

Chapter 5

NEW YORK

Bright disk-shaped lights hovered in the night sky like a fleet of flying saucers. The glowing beams were from airplanes waiting for a clear runway into the Newark, New Jersey airport. It was unearthly to see them as they were no doubt seeing us. We were gliding in slow motion as we circled New York City, twice, while waiting our turn to land. Thousands of gold lights twinkled in the city below us.

"Look! There's the Statue of Liberty!" I shouted to Autumn who was sitting right next to me. The statue's golden lights sparkled as she stood solitary, and alone. "This is so exciting!" I squealed, thinking of the fact that we were going to New York, and not what we were going there to do.

"Not for me," Autumn said.

I was sorry I had said anything. "No, not for you," I agreed.

Autumn was sitting next to the window, and she took in the sights with a different feeling. "The last time I was in New York, I was arrested," she said sadly. The pools of her ebony eyes didn't reflect the millions of lights below. Instead, they were dark with a recollection of fear and dread. "When this is over, I never want to come to New York again."

I hurriedly changed the subject. "Since we're going to be sharing a hotel room, I wanted to tell you, I'm a little bit modest. I like to change clothes in the bathroom."

"Same for me," she said.

For some reason it seemed important to get that settled. We were going to be spending a lot of time together.

Before we had left for the airport Richard advised us, saying, "Make all of your bags carry-ons. I'm afraid you're going to be bombarded with reporters at the airport. I want you to be able to make a quick exit if you need to."

It was my first trip to New York, and I had double-stuffed everything so that I would have enough clothing and shoes for the week ahead.

Autumn had dug through her grandmother's closet and came up with a decent suitcase full of changes.

When we disembarked from the plane, there wasn't any press waiting. It was a good thing, because the lengthy flight, the sleepless night before, and the far-too-heavy weight of my bags all left me feeling light-headed and hyperventilating.

"Are you okay?" Autumn asked, concern coloring her voice.

"I feel faint, and I'm not the fainting type. I better rest for a minute." I set my bags down on the floor and loosened my coat from around my throat. It would be cold outside, but I was having a sudden hot flash.

Autumn stood patiently while I pulled myself together. "Are you feeling better?" she asked after a few minutes—genuinely concerned.

"I'm just glad there wasn't any fanfare," I joked. "I could just see myself spread out on the floor and you trying to revive me. The press would love that picture."

"You better believe it," Autumn agreed as she helped me gather my bags.

We found our way outside to the cab-stand. It was ten o'clock at night. "How much is it to the Fairfield Inn in East Rutherford?" I asked a large woman in a small cubby-sized office filled with maps and schedules.

Autumn searched through her bags for the address.

"Thirty-six dollars," the woman said with disinterest, and pointed to the cab we would be taking.

As we rode along unfamiliar freeways, we trusted that the cab driver knew where he was going.

I don't think he understood a word of English, and I didn't understand a word he said. He was speaking some gibberish at us, and I asked Autumn, "What's he saying?"

"I think he's saying we're lost."

"What next?" I asked—exasperated that the driver didn't know where we were.

"Don't worry, we'll be at the hotel soon," Autumn said reassuringly.

We were both exhausted from our thirteen hours of travel.

The driver pulled into the parking lot of the seediest bar we had ever seen. He got out of the cab to ask directions.

Overhead, a half-lit gas light of a martini glass was threatening to fall off its hinges. A blue neon beer sign hung in a dirty window of the sleazy establishment. The cars in the parking lot were beat up, raked, and lowered. They were a muddy cast of colors sitting under a single lamppost in the otherwise dark parking lot.

"Oh, that's great!" I told Autumn. "Our first hour in town and here we are, like sitting ducks, just waiting for someone to come out and mug us."

"I know," Autumn said. "You would think the cab drivers would know where all the hotels are."

We locked the doors.

The driver came back. We hopelessly drove around in circles, obviously still lost.

I was losing my patience when he pulled over to a phone booth next to a torn billboard that was flapping in the wind. Before he got out of the car he was speaking garble again.

"He needs change for the phone," Autumn said.

"How did you figure that out?" I asked her as I dug for some coins.

By the time we finally arrived at the hotel, we were more than ready to call it a day. We checked in, not giving Autumn's real name.

In the hallway to our room, we could smell fresh paint. It was a delightful contrast to the stale urine-scented cab in which we had been riding.

When we walked into our room, we saw brand-new matching bedspreads on top of two double beds. "Which bed do you want?" I asked.

"I don't care."

"I'll take the one next to the window then."

By the window was a desk where I could do some writing. A dresser held a television that faced the beds.

"That's fine. I'm going to check out the stairs for a place to smoke," Autumn said. "Maybe there'll be a fire escape." She must have found one, because she came back into the room smelling like sweet-vanilla incense.

What was left of the night went by quickly and morning came too soon. We had to be in Manhattan early and we were still in Newark.

When Autumn was dressed she offered to go to the front desk and get directions. "I'll go down and see what time the bus comes." She came back carrying a handful of breakfast goodies from the lobby. She dropped a jelly-donut she was juggling, and powdered sugar left a snow flurry sprinkled on the floor.

"Come on," I said. "We'll get you another donut on the way out."

A fierce February wind was blowing and it was whipping against our faces as we stood waiting for a commuter bus to take us into the city. "I'm freezing," I told Autumn, as I pulled my old winter coat, a size too small, tighter around my middle.

"I'm not too bad," she said. "Grandma gave me some gloves to wear."

Grandma had given her everything she was wearing including the blue blazer she had on for court. I had given her a pair of earrings for the trip and they matched the jacket perfectly. They were butterflies, a reminder of the *Butterfly* in her medicine totem. "These are to remind you to rise above it all," I told her.

When the bus finally came, there was standing room only. We hung onto the carriage rack as we went through the Lincoln tunnel that runs under the Hudson River. Small streams of water trickled down the walls of the tunnel and I worried that it might collapse at any moment. Other commuter buses rallied alongside, leaving just a few inches between the vehicles. The traffic was bumper to bumper, but it continued to move, pushing its way into the city.

We were let off by a set of descending stairs leading into a huge building called the Port Authority that houses the bus-line and subway connections. We rode down one of the several stories of escalators carrying a non-ending ribbon of commuters hurrying to make their transit connections. Security officers, mostly short and stout, wore stiff-billed hats and carried nightsticks.

The smell of rancid urine mixed with the better smell of hot cinnamon buns coming from an open bakery. We left the hustle of the building, and headed for the bustling street to hail a cab.

In a few minutes we were in front of a ten-story building where Autumn's lawyer had his office. When she opened the car door, the recorded voice of sex therapist, Dr. Ruth, reminded us to make sure we had all of our packages.

"Only in New York," I told Autumn as I paid the driver through a tiny window that was extremely filthy.

ᏇᏣᏗ᷉Ꮧ

We had only waited a couple of minutes when Robert Baum walked into the waiting room from behind a locked door that was stenciled with the words *Federal Court Legal Aid Department*. "Mrs. Jesperson," he said using my married name. His hand was outstretched.

He was appropriately dressed in a dark suit and tie. He had rabbit-shaped front teeth, and a boyish grin that was in contrast to the large bulk of his body.

"Hello, Autumn," he said, reaching out to hug her.

"Hi, Robert," she said hugging him back.

He introduced us to the group of people waiting behind him.

"This is Ed Zas," Baum started. "He will be the legal counsel." Ed was also dressed in a suit. He was a Yale law student. "And, this is Debbie, our Public Investigator." Debbie was the hipster of the team. She wore a strand of hippie beads around her young twenty-something neck. Thin straight blonde hair hung loosely around her shoulders. Jessica was doing the research and would spend most of her time in the background. The common link between the three was their youthful ages.

Robert was more my age of forty-seven—him being closer to fifty. He was a temple graying New Yorker who had his hands on what would be one of the hottest cases of the year.

The headlines about Autumn ran side by side with the murder of the child, JonBenet Ramsey, which had happened less than three weeks before Autumn's arrest. Pictures of Ennis Cosby would be at her other side.

Even though Autumn was not suspected of having anything to do with Cosby's son's murder, she was surrounded by it in the press.

We were led into a conference room where Baum produced a piece of paper. He thought Autumn should make a public announcement. He handed me the paper so I could look it over. I read it and handed it to Autumn.

My husband would prefer Autumn not say anything," I told Baum.

"It would be helpful to her case if she says something."

"You're the one who will have to go home and face your uncle," I reminded her.

It was ultimately Autumn's decision, and as a compromise, she chose a couple of items from the list.

Though we had made it into the building without anyone noticing, Baum warned us that it would be different on the way over to the courthouse. In the lobby, he arranged us into a formation. I would stand on one side of Autumn, arms linked, and Baum would be on the other. The legal team would follow. "It's best not to smile,"

Baum suggested. "We want the press to know we are serious about this."

"I suffer from the smiling disease," I told him as my lips curled upwards.

"Yes, she does," Autumn confirmed.

"I'm from the country and everyone smiles there."

"For right now it wouldn't be a good idea," Baum reiterated.

"Of course," I relented, quickly losing my smile.

"Are you nervous?" I asked Autumn.

"Not really," she said sounding too relaxed.

As soon as we walked out the door we were surrounded. We didn't have to worry about smiling as we were fighting to stay standing. We were being shoved from every direction.

"Autumn, why do you think Cosby is your father?" someone in the crowd of reporters asked.

"Autumn, do you have anything to say?" asked another.

"Autumn, how are you doing?"

The stream of questions was endless. Not only were we not to smile, Autumn had been instructed not to say anything until after her court hearing.

The reporters worked in teams, three to a group. The television anchors held microphones pointed in Autumn's direction. The cameramen kept their cameras pointed at Autumn as they walked backwards. Spotters walked behind them to be the eyes at the back of their heads. "Car! Pole! Step up . . . Look out!" they shouted, while moving camera wires and lines that might trip someone up.

Cars honked ceaselessly when we disturbed the heavy traffic flow to get across to the old majestic courthouse.

The reflective lenses of the cameras were inches from our faces, and we couldn't see where we were going. We were being directed by the casing of bodies surrounding us. One reporter, a woman with thick wavy brown hair, asked non-stop questions. I had my elbow pressed against her chest in an attempt to keep her away from Autumn.

Autumn was the eye of a media-tornado, and she marched on, quiet and calm, amid the total chaos of the crowd.

At the courthouse steps, several policemen restrained the cameramen from following any further. A couple of the reporters were let by, but without their cameras.

We filed through a glass and brass revolving door that spun as smooth as a merry-go-round. Inside the building was a whole different climate. The cool marble floors instilled a hushed silence. Everyone kept their voices low. We removed our coats to a conveyer belt and walked through a security scan.

In an ancient elevator, Baum gave us a formal introduction to Susan who worked for *Hard Copy*. She was the one who had become intimate with my elbow. She refrained from her barrage of questions, somehow knowing that it was off limits now that we were inside. She was almost apologetic as she told us, "It's my job to ask questions."

Still, she took the opportunity to pitch Autumn for an interview in a less challenging manner than she had presented outside. "I want everyone to have a chance to hear your side," she said as if she were an ally.

We walked into a crowded courtroom, and Baum found us a couple of seats. Autumn was quietly composed. She didn't appear to be nervous, but her insides had to be shaking. Mine were shaking for her.

Silver butterflies dangled from the blue crystals that made up Autumn's earrings. "Just remember the butterflies," I reminded her and patted her on the back. "You look nice," I said, trying to boost her confidence.

Five sketch artists were in the room. They hadn't missed our entrance. Clipped to their glasses were small pairs of binoculars, giving them the appearance of having a double set of eyes. They were focusing on Autumn's face.

One of the artists came over to us. She was part of an unmistakable mother-daughter team. The two women both had long, blonde, unkempt hair.

They were dressed in artist casual, with chalk on their shirts and pant legs. The dowdy daughter was standing to the side of me, and I peered over her giant clipboard to see what she was drawing. Her picture didn't look anything like Autumn, and I said so. She looked hurt, but she didn't miss a beat. Her pastels continued to rub across the pad. "Did you do the picture that came out in the paper?" I asked her.

"Yes," she said, lighting up a bit.

A few people who hadn't been able to find seats were standing and watching the pear-shaped artist as she worked on Autumn's picture.

"Would you draw me next," a man asked.

"You're not famous enough," she said.

"Autumn, could you turn your face this way a little?" the artist asked unabashedly.

Autumn moved her head to accommodate the woman, but she never changed her solemn expression.

Just before Autumn's turn to go before the judge, I told her, "It's going to be okay. Just remember to breathe."

She gave me a weak smile.

Yosie was brought in. He was small of stature, had dyed red hair, and wore a Jewish Kippah. Autumn joined him at a table on the other side of the gate, but she never looked at him.

The presiding judge asked Autumn, "How do you plead?"

"Not guilty," she told him clearly, and then she was ushered back to her seat.

A wooden box much like the one BINGO numbers are pulled from, sat on the judge's desk. The box held the names of the judges who would take the different cases once the indictments were in place.

When Autumn's name came up, Baum was next to us. The squirrel cage whirled around, and I couldn't help but think of Russian roulette. Autumn's fate was spinning in front of us.

The judge reached in the box and pulled out the name, Barbara Jones.

Baum smiled. "She's okay," he said sounding relieved.

The judges' reputations preceded them. When the next person's judge was announced, friends and family cringed. A communal groan was heard around the room, and then we left.

At the bottom of the courthouse steps, a sawhorse barricade had been set up. More cameras and crews had joined the troupes. Cameramen were standing at eye level, while other members of their teams were crouched down in front. They were holding microphones to capture the audio. Some of the members of the press were holding cameras and were snapping repetitive pictures. A clump of microphones had been taped together at the center of the bright yellow boundary. They were plugged into their respective satellite-adorned vans lining the street. The reporters could have come around the wooden structure easily enough, but they played by a loose rule of journalistic etiquette. For now they were subdued as they were waiting to hear the headline news of the moment.

I stood off to the side while Baum and Autumn walked up to the makeshift podium.

"I deny the charges that have been brought against me," Autumn said, quoting from Baum's list. "I would like to send my condolences to the Cosby family about Ennis's death." She enunciated her words, making them sound a bit forced.

"I think the evidence at trial will prove she is Bill Cosby's daughter," Baum said.

The investigator, Debbie, tapped him on the shoulder, and he turned to leave. By the time I reached Autumn the reporters were swarming in around us, and havoc reigned again. I could see they would easily squeeze me out to get at Autumn. She was my charge and I wasn't going to let that happen. With only the second try at it, I was holding my own much better.

"Autumn, how do you plan to prove Cosby is your father?" a reporter shouted.

The incessant questions bombarded our ears along with the other shouts and noises coming from the street's non-ending rush hour.

Chapter 6

FULL MOON

It was a beautiful day to be in New York City. Even though the wind was still blowing it had warmed up considerably. The street was remarkably clear of all reporters. The photographers were busy developing their pictures of Autumn, and Baum offered to take us to lunch. We walked several blocks to the "Little Italy" section of Manhattan. We talked as we strolled down the crowded avenues past sidewalk cafes and curio shops—the defense team in tow.

"The toughest part of the defense will be the amount of the extortion, ahem, the forty million," Baum shared.

"What about Tony?" I asked. "He's on the prosecution's side."

"That too," Baum replied.

At lunch, Autumn answered everyone's questions, but she didn't volunteer any extra information.

"This is the way I think we should approach the defense," Ed said. He told Autumn about court rulings that could help argue her case.

"How was your flight?" Debbie asked, lightening things up a bit.

"It was fine," Autumn replied unanimated.

"How is your mother?" Baum asked.

"Same ol'," Autumn answered. "She calls me every day."

After lunch Baum insisted he buy us some New York pastries. We walked into one of his favorite bakeries. The delicacies were beyond compare. Everything was full of cream and decorated to perfection.

"Oh, look Autumn!" I pulled her over to see a glazed fruit tart that sparkled with a crystallized sugar coating, and the cheesecake called to be eaten.

"Do you like cheesecake?" I asked her.

"Not that much, but this looks good," she said, pointing out a caramel laced dessert.

Baum had cannoli and other tasty morsels packed into a pink box and then tied with a white-cotton string. "These are for you to take back to the hotel," he said, handing Autumn the boxed goodies.

When we were back at Baum's office, it was time to work on the case. Autumn and I went into the conference room with the legal team.

"I'll join you later," Baum told us. "I have some calls to make."

Autumn had agreed that I would write a book about what was happening so I was able to sit in and take notes. She also informed Baum that I would be writing a book about the trial. He offered to provide copies of whatever I needed. I had just started out as a writer and Autumn agreed it would be a worthy first book. She had no interest in writing a book herself.

"Tell us what happened, Autumn," Debbie directed.

I took out my pad and paper, determined to write an accurate account of the story.

"From the beginning?" Autumn asked.

"Sure."

"I met Yosie at the hotel where I worked," she started. "He flattered me a lot. He would tell me, 'This is what I'll do for you . . .'"

Autumn's voice was young—fragile. Her hands moved in jesters over the cool tabletop—mapping out her thoughts.

"*Down on the Farm. . .* was supposed to be sold to a children's programming station for eighty thousand dollars. Tony was supposed to get twenty percent. I was going to share his percentage. We were going to use it as a down payment on a house we found."

"Yosie was prone to a lot of temper fits," Autumn went on. "When my mother kicked us out, Yosie said he would get in touch with Mr. Cosby. At the end of December, I used the private answering-service number I had for Mr. Cosby. I left a message for him to call me. I talked to my mother, and she told me Mr. Cosby would be calling. She also told me, she had told him not to give me any money. Mr. Cosby called around midnight, and I told him I was homeless." She accentuated the word "homeless."

"'This is what I'm going to do,' he said. 'I'll pay for your education and give you two hundred dollars a week for living expenses.' He told me when I was enrolled in school to get back to him. He would pay for all my tuition and books, but I had to keep a *B* average and work at a job at least eight hours a week. I asked him, what am I supposed to do until then? He asked me how much I needed, and I told him two thousand dollars would be good. He told me to go to the Philip Morris agency the next day, and ask for this guy whose name I can't remember right now. Then he said, 'I understand that you've been telling people that I'm your father; you don't need to be telling your friends this.' I told him I hadn't told anyone. The next day I picked up a fed-ex at Phillip Morris. Inside was three thousand dollars instead of the two thousand that had been agreed on."

"What did you do with the cash?" Ed asked.

"Tony and I put some of it on a hotel room, and then we bought a word-processor."

"What was the word-processor for?"

"So we could type letters and stuff. We worked morning until night for Yosie on the show."

"When we ran out of money again, we asked Yosie if we could stay with him, but he said we couldn't. We asked for an advance, but he said we wouldn't get any money until the show sold. When we asked him what we should do, he said, 'Call Cosby.' Yosie told me it was okay to call a tabloid with my story. He told Tony and me that he could protect me by having me sign the rights of my story over to him. He said, 'I'll write your life story, and you can sell it.' Yosie told me he had checked with some lawyers he knew and that we weren't doing anything illegal. He told me to call some lawyers as well. I called a couple of lawyers' offices and they told me I was too old to get back child support. I tried to call Mr. Cosby, but he wouldn't take my calls, so I called Jack Schmitt. He handled the trust accounts that Mr. Cosby set up for my mother and for me."

"When I called Jack I could hear something funny in his voice and I told him, 'You're acting like I'm doing something wrong. It's not fair that I have to sleep in my car."

"Yosie felt it was important that we make the powers-that-be aware of the way I was being treated. He dictated letters to the President, Vice President, and Jessie Jackson. He was looking for discrimination support. He put in a paragraph about 'deadbeat fathers' and I asked him why he did that. We argued about it for quite a while. In the end, I surrendered. I was tired of fighting with him. Around January 15th, Yosie called the *Globe* and told them he had a story about a girl who was Cosby's daughter. The *Globe* offered twelve thousand dollars for the story, but Yosie said we should hold out for fifty thousand. He wanted half of the money for himself. Yosie would make sexual innuendoes toward me, and he was abusive. I just wanted to get away from him. I wanted to get rid of all the watchdogs in my life. I was tired of everyone holding something over me. When I was younger, I asked Mr. Cosby, 'Do you understand how it is not to know your father?'"

"I don't know about everyone else," I jumped in, "but I'm exhausted." Autumn's deposition had been going on for over two hours.

It was getting dark out, and I was eager to return to the hotel.

"I'm having trouble keeping my thoughts straight," Autumn confessed, leaning her tired head toward the table.

"Go ahead to Baum's office," Debbie said. "We can continue tomorrow."

When we went to Baum's office, he was just getting off the phone.

"Look at all of this," Baum said, pointing to a desktop spread with pink memo-notes. "These are from people wanting interviews. Just tell me who you would like to do an interview with, and I'll set it up." He picked up one note after another reading off the names of recognizable newspaper and television tabloids. "Susan from *Hard Copy* would like you to give her a short interview over the phone," Baum said to Autumn.

"This is our first day in New York and we have only had a few hours of sleep, not to mention jet lag," I groaned.

I was hoping Autumn would say something in agreement, but her mind was wandering elsewhere.

"This is part of it," Baum said. "If I help them out, they help me out. You understand." He let loose a big rabbit grin.

The phone rang and it was Susan. "Look," said Baum putting her on hold. "I told her she could pitch you, but you don't have to say anything if you don't want to."

I had come to the city to be Autumn's protector and guardian. I was ready to protect her from her own lawyer if need be. "We're ready to go home now," I said.

"It's okay," Autumn said calmly in my direction. She turned to Baum. "I don't have to say anything, right?"

"Right," said Baum.

"Okay then."

"I'll put Susan on the loud speaker," Baum said clicking the conference button on the phone.

"Ot'umn, Ot'umn, are you there?" Susan asked with a thick English accent.

Autumn sat silently.

"She's here," Baum said. "Go ahead."

Susan's pleading for an interview felt endless, but was probably no longer than five minutes. "I want you to have a chance to tell your side of the story," she repeated from the afternoon elevator ride.

While Susan had been talking, I noticed a picture sitting on a table behind Baum. It was of a good-looking redheaded woman. When the call ended I asked Baum, "Is that your wife?"

"Yes," he answered.

"She's beautiful," I complimented.

"She looks like you," Autumn said.

I laughed it off, but there were similarities.

Baum rode the subway with us to the Port Authority.

After an hour of commuting, we made it back to the hotel.

"I'm going for a smoke," Autumn told me. After picking up a half-smoked vanilla cigar she headed out the door.

I stretched out on the bed.

When Autumn came back, a sweet aroma preceded her. She turned on the television and there we were walking across the screen.

"On, my gosh," I said sitting up. "They don't waste any time. We were just in court this morning!"

"No, they don't," Autumn responded.

She was not interested in watching the scene and went to change the channel.

"No, wait, it will be over in a minute, I want to hear what they have to say."

A full-face shot of Autumn was given while they replayed the statement she had made earlier behind the barricades. The butterfly earrings fluttered about when she moved her head.

"Autumn Jackson appeared in court today, wearing butterfly earrings," a reporter said.

"Autumn, they're talking about the earrings I made you. What a trip!"

"Yeah, you'd think they'd have better things to talk about."

"I wonder what they think the butterflies mean."

"It's hard to say," she said complacently.

"Are you hungry?" I asked, realizing she wasn't interested in pursuing the news topic. "We can order in."

"I'm starving!" she said. She fished through the nightstand that separated the beds and found the local restaurant menus. "They have Chinese," she said.

We ordered Italian, and started a nightly tradition. We would try all the delivering establishments we had menus for, before we left.

Autumn found a sitcom to watch, and we munched out like two teenagers. The only interruption to the evening would be the flashes of Cosby on his network station, or one of his JELL-O commercials would come on reminding us of why we were in New York in the first place.

I was the first to fall asleep. Autumn had more of a nocturnal nature than I did. I was an early riser while she liked sleeping in. She would stay up at least until midnight every night.

Come morning, I would be the first one in the bathroom, allowing her some extra sleep. She looked so angelic tucked under the blankets. In the early morning hours she looked as peaceful as any sleeping child. The vision reminded me of Autumn when she was a teenager. She had been eager about life—excited at the possibilities. She even had her career thought out in detail. "I'm going to be an architect," she had told me many times.

However, Autumn didn't have any emotional support for her dreams. Cosby was a fantasy dad, a sitcom dad, who couldn't give her a hug through the television. I wondered what imaginary conversations she might have had with him while she laid in her bed at night. How many times must she have practiced what she would say the first time she saw him face to face?

The next day we headed into the city at our leisure. We took the subway to the World Trade Center.

Autumn had been there before with her grandmother, and she gave me a quick guided tour. They had stayed at the Trade Center's hotel when she went to meet Cosby for the first time. She had been seventeen when she finally was able to meet with him eye to eye.

Autumn and I made our way to Chinatown. A novel part of New York City, Chinatown was filled with the same sights and smells as the Orient. There were mysteries to be discovered at every vegetable stand. We enjoyed watching the live turtles at the fish markets. We didn't dwell on the fact that they were there to be sold as a meal.

"They're all trying to get to the top," Autumn observed as their tiny finned feet scratched across the backs of the other captives.

I was starting to fade with hunger. "Where do you want to have lunch?" I asked Autumn.

"At a nice restaurant," she replied.

A marquee hung over our heads. It read: *Nice Restaurant*.

We looked at each other and laughed.

"This must be the place," Autumn said.

42

We walked through a doorway leading to a set of stairs.

As we crested the top, we saw a "nice" restaurant full of Chinese people.

"They know where the good food is," I said, reassuring her as we both took the final steps of commitment. We made our way to a far corner table that was by a coat rack.

We were brought tea and menus, one side was written in Chinese, and the other was in English. "I'm going to order the "Buddha Special," I told Autumn. "It looks like a 'nice' mix of vegetables."

A cart was being pushed around that held steaming appetizers.

"No thanks," we said in answer to the Mandarin spoken invitation.

"If I eat snacks, I won't eat the meal," Autumn said.

I kept trying to flag a waiter down, but the waiters would only come so close and then walk off in the other direction.

Autumn was laughing at my feeble attempts to draw their attention.

I finally caught a waiter who could no longer ignore my hand waving and wispy whistles.

"We're ready to order," I said, feeling in control at last.

He said something in Mandarin and then left.

A few minutes later the cart was coming our way again.

At first we declined, but then we realized we might not ever get lunch if we didn't order at least one thing from the wagon. Just to be on the safe side, we ordered two dishes of strange looking finger foods.

When my Buddha Special showed up, I nearly lost Autumn under the table she was laughing so hard.

The waiter had brought a huge pie dish filled three inches high with noodles, vegetables, and an assortment of mushrooms. It looked delightful, but even a hungry man would have been intimidated.

"I can just see you trying to eat all of that," Autumn said laughing hysterically.

Her laughter had a ring to it. It came from a place of child-like innocence and joy. Her laugh was one of her charms.

Things really got out of hand when I went to pay the check and accidentally tore a hundred-dollar bill in two, right in front of the waiter. It had caught on the side of my wallet. I sheepishly handed him the two parts.

"I guess I didn't want to let go of the money," I said. When he walked away with the pieces, we were both in stitches.

"You're too much," Autumn said in jest.

Once we were outside, we walked toward Baum's office to make Autumn's two o'clock appointment.

Autumn stopped at a sidewalk vendor's stand. "How much is this hat?" she asked. She didn't have much money with her, but she was going to take Tony back a leather cap. She had already priced several of them.

We came up on a large African American woman who must have been six feet tall. She was talking loudly to her friends. "I'll kill the bitch," she said, not caring who heard her.

"People are really uptight in New York," I observed.

Just then an angry cabby honked his horn.

"Living here gets to you after a while," Autumn confirmed.

Without realizing it, we had walked right up on a Channel 10 van. Again we witnessed some weird journalistic etiquette. The reporter and cameraman just waved when they recognized Autumn. I had half expected that they would jump out of the van and run after us.

We were nearly to Baum's office when we heard a man shouting, "One dolla'! One dolla'!"

A huddle surrounded a corner vendor, and we ventured over to see what he had. Two large crates were stuffed with sweaters, most of them in plastic bags.

"Are all the sweaters a dollar?" I asked.

The vendor looked at me and nodded in recognition that I had asked what should have been obvious. I was wasting his time.

Autumn threw a sweater my way. "That one looks like you," she said.

I had four sweaters in my arms and was digging for more when Autumn came up next to me. "We have to go," she said.

"Okay, I'm almost done."

"You don't understand," Autumn said seriously. "Someone has recognized me and she's getting loud about it."

A plump African American woman was yelling to her friends, "Look, there's Cosby's daughter!" She was headed in our direction.

We paid for what we held and quickly walked away.

"I didn't mind that she recognized me, but she was yelling about it," Autumn said.

"I guess you'll have to get used to this," I told her.

It sparked fear in us though. Our hearts were beating hard and our adrenaline was pumping. We looked into the eyes of every one who was passing us as if they were secret enemies.

After all the unwelcome excitement, we had missed a turn and ended up on Nassau Street that was closed for a Friday sale day.

We saw a shop that had discount coats, and we vowed to come back.

We both needed better coats for the freezing New York winter weather.

Street music lured us in its direction. In San Francisco it would have been a protest that drew such a crowd, but it was nothing more than a half dozen African American kids beating on pots and pans, and sounding quite good at it too. We skirted the crowd, and found our way to Baum's Duane Street office.

After cordial hellos Autumn continued with her deposition.

"We sent a fax to Jack Schmitt," Autumn started. "A letter was sent telling him I needed money. Later that day, Yosie told us that Ennis had been killed. I was shocked because I didn't know Mr. Cosby had a son. I thought he had all daughters. When Jack called about 3:00 p.m. to make a deal, I told him I was upset that no one had told me about Ennis. He didn't want to talk about Ennis. He changed the subject saying I was going to get the money but forty million was too much. I told him I would call him back. Yosie told me to meet Jack half way. When I called Jack back, we agreed on twenty-four million. He told me to come to New York to pick it up. I told him I would need plane tickets for Yosie and me. He said he would send them. Yosie asked me how much of a cut he was going to get. I told him twenty percent, the same amount he was offering us for working on the production. That wasn't enough for Yosie. He played on our sympathies by saying, 'I think of you as my children.' We settled on twenty five percent."

It was dark by the time Autumn and I headed back to New Jersey. We were both tired from all the walking, and Autumn was drained from the intense period of questioning. We were a few minutes past our bus stop when we realized we had missed getting off at the right place.

I told the driver what had happened, and he told us to get off and wait for a bus that would be coming the other way. "It should only be a few minutes," he said. He gave us transfers and let us off the bus.

We balanced our packages, holding the sweaters and other goods we had picked up during the day, and walked across the deserted street to the marked bus stop.

The few minutes turned into a very long wait. Autumn took the opportunity for a smoke.

Every now and then a car would drive by. Whoever was driving would slow down and look us over. The drivers were faceless silhouettes in their darkened cars.

"They probably think we're hookers," Autumn said.

"Yeah, hookers, that like to shop!" I said, shifting my bundles.

We looked up at the full moon taunting us, and sneering at us through thin translucent clouds.

"I don't think we should tell the guys about this adventure," I said.

"No, we'd better not," Autumn agreed. "They would just worry about us even more."

It was a good half-hour before we saw the bus we were waiting for come into view.

The next day Baum picked us up for a tour of Manhattan. We cruised Fifth Avenue, and passed by the Empire State Building. "Do you want to go up?" Balm asked.

"Not today," I said. I was enjoying just riding around and seeing everything. When we returned home Autumn turned on the news and it was being reported that a maniac gunman had killed several tourists at the top of the Empire State Building around the time we were passing by. I considered it a good omen that we had forewent the tourist attraction.

Over lunch we discussed what would be helpful for Autumn's case.

"During the trial don't wear much makeup," Baum suggested. He wanted to play up her innocent youthful look. She already had a young demeanor and didn't wear much makeup anyway. I would always forget that she was past being a teenager until she reached for her cigars.

Chapter 7

TORRENTIAL TEARS

How quickly we become creatures of habit. As soon as Autumn and I would arrive back at the hotel, Autumn would smoke a cigar and I would write in my journal. Then we would watch the current events about Autumn on the national news. After that, we would look for a good movie as a diversion from why we were holed up together in a hotel room so far from home.

Alcohol was not something that had been an area of concern in Autumn's life or mine, but under duress, we had both taken to having a cocktail at night as a way to relax from the hectic day and hopefully fall asleep a little bit easier. I had brought a flask of brandy from home. Autumn preferred vodka but didn't have any with her so we needed to find the appropriate store.

Shopping in New York was so different from shopping in California. In New York City everything was extremely specialized, just food in the food store, just hardware at the hardware store, etc. "I like California better, where everything is lumped together in super markets," I told Autumn.

"Everything is separated here," Autumn said agreeing. We had practically given up on finding the elusive repository, when she saw a narrow shop window that held various types of beverages including hard liquor.

"Here we are!" Autumn said, perking up.

"I would like a small bottle of vodka, please," Autumn told an old man behind the counter.

"I'll need to see some identification," he said cautiously. He laid his wrinkled hands on the counter and leaned forward. His graying hair was disheveled, and he looked more like he should be in the country than the city. He was wearing a faded flannel shirt.

Autumn barely looked sixteen so it was natural that she would be carded. She produced her driver's license.

Begrudgingly, as if her license had been lying, he handed her a small bottle of over-priced Russian vodka.

It was the day after Autumn had gone to court. On the way home, I asked Autumn, "Doesn't it bother you that Tony hasn't called to see how things went in court?" Richard had called a couple of times and I was surprised that Tony hadn't.

"No, he'll call eventually," she said, sounding secure in their relationship. "Something must have come up."

Beside Autumn's mother, Tony's sister Camilla was the only person to do a paid interview. She was supposed to use part of the money to clear Autumn's bad checks. She would give Tony money for living expenses, and then keep the rest. Everyone was agreeable to the arrangement.

Camilla told *Hard Copy's* Jodi Baskerville that she didn't think Tony or Autumn were bad people. She knew they were very much in love and had wanted to get married.

Autumn and I had each poured ourselves a drink when the phone rang.

"Hi Rony (rhymes with Tony)," Autumn chirped, calling him by her special pet name.

In less than a minute she was laughing joyfully, temporarily forgetting her woes.

As their conversation ran on, she became more serious.

"Yes . . . okay. . . I understand . . . okay, I'll talk to you later then . . . I love you."

Autumn placed the phone back in the cradle and looked up at me despairingly. "Tony just told me his sister is not going to be able to pay the twelve hundred dollar fee for my warrant."

Baum had made it clear that it was a priority for Autumn to take care of her warrant in Florida, and as soon as possible.

"Clearing your warrant should've been taken care of before Camilla spent money on anything else," I told Autumn.

"Camilla bought a car, and then Tony needed some money."

I was outraged that Tony's sister had made money over Autumn's crisis, and then not used a dime of it to help her out. I was even more upset that Tony had taken money, though I didn't know how much, from his sister without helping Autumn first.

I couldn't talk to Tony and Camilla about their choices, so it was Autumn I turned to with my anxiety.

"You told me Tony's sister was going to take care of your bad checks."

"She told me she would pay the fines. She was supposed to get paid ten thousand dollars for the interview."

"You can't expect Richard to take care of this, too," I said. "He bailed you out at the risk of everything we own, and it's not like we're young enough to start over. I think he's already done more than enough."

"I never asked to be bailed out," Autumn sputtered in defiance.

When Autumn and I left for New York, Richard had given Tony money to fly home to Florida and see his family. At the time, Tony wasn't sure if he was coming back to California.

"Tony should stay in Florida until your debt is paid," I said. "He needs to get a job and help you through this."

"There aren't any jobs in Florida."

"It would be easier for him to get a job there where he knows people and can make connections. What's he going to do in Lake County where he doesn't know anyone and jobs are also scarce?"

"Everyone keeps blaming Tony for everything," she said, completely missing my point.

"I didn't say anything against Tony. What I said was that he needs to help you out, and get your checks paid off. Who do you expect to pay your debt?"

"I will," she said.

"And how are you going to do that?"

"I'll get a job."

"Show me!"

"I will!"

"Good!"

After pouring another drink I said, "Tony should stay with his family. It's not fair to ask Lois to take him in, too. Your living with her is one thing, but with Tony there, three will be a crowd."

"I'm going to marry Tony," she said. Teardrops sprouted up at the corners of Autumn's eyes as she held up the engagement ring from Tony.

Ironically, Richard had given me an identical ring for a ten-year anniversary present.

"What do you think this is?" she said, pointing to a straight row of variegated diamonds. Her face scrunched up, and her shoulders crumbled. She ran into the bathroom and locked the door.

I could hear her sobbing so much that she was gasping for breath.

Suddenly, I was quite sober and hoping that with all she was facing, that she wouldn't take a razor blade to her wrists. The vision frightened me.

"Autumn, please unlock the door," I pleaded. "We need to talk."

I retreated to my bed, and was sorry that I had lost control. Everything felt impossible, critical, and unmanageable.

Eventually, the loud weeping subsided, and Autumn unlocked the latch to the door.

"Thank God," I thought to myself.

When she came out and sat on her bed, I went to her.

"I'm so sorry. I lost my faith that everything is as it should be," I said. "This whole thing has been so difficult; it came at us out of nowhere and turned our lives upside down."

"It's going to be over for you and Richard though," she said. "I could be going to prison."

"But, we didn't do anything to bring this on ourselves. You did."

"It's all I can do to deal with what has happened," Autumn moaned, slightly hiccupping from her tears.

"I know," I told her. I put my arm around her and gave her a maternal kiss on the cheek. I touched the hair at the back of her head as if she were my own child. "I'll stand by you until this is over," I said, meaning it. "We're both tired, let's get some sleep."

"Okay," she said flatly.

I chided myself, and before being silent I said, "I'll try not to worry so much."

"Goodnight," she said. Her voice deep with exhaustion.

§☾✦☽♭

Autumn and I seemed to instinctually know our roles as aunt and niece. One of my chores was to be the timekeeper. "It's time to get up," I told Autumn.

I could only see a spray of black hair against a white pillowslip.

When she didn't respond, I burst into a song I used to sing my children first thing in the morning to get them up out of bed. *"Rise and shine, and sing out the glory, glory. . ."*

"Ooooo," cooed Autumn, coming out of her cozy cocoon in a full stretch. She looked at me oddly, not knowing what to think of my off-key singing.

When Autumn was done in the bathroom, I asked, "How did you sleep?" Still feeling bad about the night before, I was making sure to be extra attentive. She needed my support, not my panic.

"Pretty good," she said. "But, I had a nightmare about my mother. I dreamt we were having a fight."

"That's understandable," I said. "You and I were fighting last night, and you've been trying to break away from your mother. Your dream was most likely about growing pains."

"That's probably it," Autumn said. "I'm going down for some breakfast."

"I'll come with you."

We rode the elevator to the lobby and there were two counters full of continental-style breakfast foods. A coffee maker, a toaster, and a microwave were all in a row. Several plastic tables and chairs were set up for the hotel guests. A large screen television was at one end of the room.

Just as we were about to sit down, the morning news came on, and there was Autumn's face filling the screen. The next scene was the two of us walking down the steps of the court building on the day the indictment had been read.

We looked at each other, as those who were eating breakfast looked at us.

Without a word, we stood up and went back to our room.

"I'm not a fighter," I told Autumn. Giving my sun sign as confirmation of this I said, "It is really unusual for me to fight about anything. Libras are lovers, not fighters. We are the peacemakers. I don't want to argue with you."

"Me either," Autumn said coolly.

"When you have to go to trial, we'll get a place that has at least one bedroom so we can have some space from each other."

"Could we get a two bedroom place?" she asked.

"Sure, if we can find one at the right price, but even one bedroom will give us a door to close between us."

"That would be good."

"The important thing to remember is that we've been together 24 hours a day for almost a week. Except for last night, we've done great. I'll try to have more faith. I know you don't need me freaking out with everything else that's going on."

"That's for sure!" Autumn said in agreement.

We turned our focus to the business at hand, and I assumed that we were still friends.

We rode the commuter bus to the Port Authority, and then rode down the four flights of escalators to the underground subway station.

One of Autumn's responsibilities was to be the keeper of the tokens needed to ride the trains. She searched her purse and handed me a brass coin that would free the turnstile.

The mix of people who rode the subway reflected the general population who lived in the city. Mothers, children, prostitutes, thieves, and preachers, were just some of the populous who rode the underground all-metal coaches.

I cringed when I saw a suited man reading the paper. I said to Autumn, "I wonder how long it will take him to figure out you're the one on the front page."

"Oh, I'm sure he'll figure it out."

The man looked at us directly over the top of his reading glasses. He saw us looking at him, and he looked back to his paper.

"He's made the connection," Autumn said. She was becoming more comfortable with her infamy and didn't make any attempt to move.

When we arrived at Baum's office, he had us join him in the conference room. A well-worn book sat in front of him. "This is the sentencing guidelines book," Baum said, flipping through the many hundreds of pages with his thumb.

He looked up the section for extortion. "Points are added for the caliber of the crime. It's the large amount of money asked for that is working against you adding up to, let me see . . . twelve years in prison. That's the most you could get," Baum said as gently as possible. "The judges rule pretty much by the book, so you're looking at a minimum of five years. The only other alternative I can think of is a boot-camp situation I might be able to arrange. In that case, you would be out in six months. There's no guarantee that will happen though."

This time we treated Baum to lunch. We went to a neighborhood bar and grill. We swallowed our pasta with the ill news of just how much trouble Autumn was facing.

Earlier that morning, we had been at court for a gag order to be set in place. It would keep the defense from finding out just how much Bill was worth financially. We went through the same media frenzy and pointed questions as the time before.

When we passed by a newspaper stand that afternoon I said, "Look Autumn, you're on the front page of every paper." I stopped to buy one of each.

"You would think they would put important news on the front pages," she said, unaffected.

On our way to the subway, a good looking African American man walked by and said, "Hello, Autumn." Some people were pointing, and others were wondering why we looked so familiar.

The next morning we packed our bags to head home. "I'm going to check my bags this time," I told Autumn.

"Me, too."

"If there are any reporters at the Sacramento airport, I'm sure Richard can pick up our things."

It was after the plane took off that Autumn told me, "Tony is going to connect with us in Missouri."

"When did you find that out?" I asked.

"Last night when he called," she said.

"Why didn't you tell me then?"

"Tony can do whatever he wants," she said. "He's a grown man."

When we made our layover stop at the St. Louis airport, I called Richard and told him to leave Autumn's grandmother at home so that when he picked us up there would be enough room in the car.

When we spotted Tony he was standing at the check-in counter for the connecting flight. He had a travel case containing a fishing pole. When Tony saw us he came running over. "Look!" he exclaimed. "The guy giving out boarding passes put me in first class. Jewel would you like to switch tickets so I can sit with Autumn?"

"That won't be a problem," I said, laughing light-heartedly. "I think we could use a break from each other after being together non-stop for a whole week."

While Autumn sat in the back of the plane telling Tony about our fight, I sat in the front of the plane sharing my frustration with my notebook. I absolutely wanted to be the best aunt ever, but it was hard when I was watching my own life unraveling. The things I had built my life around were falling away. I didn't want to quit going to school, but it would come to that. Every day there were more costs and more problems. There had certainly been no intention by Autumn to hurt us, or create upheaval in our lives. It was an unfortunate situation for all of us, and it was going to take some adjusting.

I told Richard about the fight with Autumn when we returned home, and the next day he called a family meeting.

"It's best to hash this stuff out in the open," Richard said.

Lois, Richard, Autumn and I sat around the dining table at Lois's house. Tony stood behind Autumn.

"I'm a very giving person," Autumn said.

"Yes, you are," Lois agreed.

"I'm not like my mother," Autumn continued.

"No, you're not," Lois conspired.

"Be quiet, mother," Richard said. "Go on, Autumn."

"Jewel said I'm with Tony just for the sex, but that's not true," she said, teary-eyed.

"We're going to get married," Tony added.

"That's fine if you want to get married when this is all over, but right now we just need to get through this. Autumn needs to get through this," I told Tony, turning to face him.

"That's right," Richard said. "We need to get through this. I don't care who has the biggest booger. We need to stick together."

"I'm sorry about the fight," I said apologizing to Autumn once again, and I meant it.

When it was time to leave, Autumn and I exchanged hugs. "I'll do my best to be a better aunt to you," I whispered.

I did do better for the most part, but if there was one thing I was learning through all of this it was that none of us are all perfectly good, and none of us are all perfectly bad, but rather we are all somewhere in between. That included Cosby, Autumn, her mother Shawn, and even me—Aunt Jewel.

Chapter 8

MORE ARRESTS

The campfire danced in timeless innocence. Mesmerizing gold flames licked the air, warming our dinner foursome against an early spring night.

"This has all happened before," Tony said in an attempt to philosophize. "Nothing is new. There were even planes before."

No one asked where the planes were.

"Another marshmallow?" I asked, offering Tony the bag.

Lois had found Autumn a job as a caretaker of mentally retarded adults. She was going to be staying on location overnight.

"How is your job going?" I asked Autumn.

She was wearing a fitted pair of brown jeans and a white shirt. Her feet had been laced into new tennis shoes. Lois was doing her best to outfit her, lending her own clothes, and buying Autumn what she could. She was working with mentally disabled adults as well, and her salary only went so far.

"Pretty good," Autumn said. "Some of the people I take care of are really a trip. This one guy is jerking off every morning when I go in to give him his meds."

"What do you do about that?" I asked.

"Nothing, I just pretend I don't notice," she replied.

"I don't know how you can do that kind of work. I couldn't. It's wonderful that you can."

"I don't mind it," Autumn said.

"Autumn, I want you to know that I'm very proud of you for doing what you said you would," I told her, referring to her commitment to pay off her bad checks.

Richard stoked the fire, making it snap and dance in a zealous fashion.

"How is it for you to stay alone with Lois?" I asked Tony.

"It's okay. Autumn gets to come home on the weekends, and we see each other every day."

Tony and Autumn shared a cigar and the honeyed aroma mixed with the smoky essence of the burning wood.

When it was time for them to head back to Lois's, we all shared hugs.

Things were mended between us and we were all on our best behavior.

The next day brought a new turn of events in the case.

I called Autumn. "Did you hear that Boris has been arrested?" I asked.

"Robert (Baum) told me," she said.

"You told me he didn't have anything to do with this."

"He didn't. He just gave Yosie and me a ride to the airport."

"It's hard to believe he would be arrested just for giving you a ride."

"I know, but he wasn't around for most of what was going on. He was just there to work on the kids' show. Yosie told him we needed a ride to the airport, so he gave us one."

During our next dinner together, I asked Tony the same question and basically received the same answer. "Boris gave Autumn and Yosie a ride to the airport. I don't think he knew what was going on because he wasn't there for the conversations concerning Cosby."

I took the opportunity to tell Tony that I had talked to Baum about the Witness Protection Program when Autumn and I were in New York. "Baum said that they can't find any reason for you to be on the program. They couldn't find any of the bank accounts you were talking about, or anything on the money laundering."

"Yosie covered everything up," Tony said. "He's a powerful man, and he has a lot of connections."

"Maybe this was just an opportunist situation because of Autumn's connection to Bill," I suggested.

"No!" Tony said with conviction. "There were too many plans, too much investigation on Yosie's part. We didn't tell him Cosby was Autumn's dad, but he knew it."

"Maybe someone else told him," Richard offered.

"No, because we even checked with Shawn. Yosie knew all kinds of things about Shawn, and Lois too. We don't know how he knew, but he said he spent a lot of time talking to Bill on the phone."

"Were you ever there when he was talking to him?" I asked.

"No," said Autumn. "He would talk to him after we left for the day."

"Yosie told us that Bill was adopted and that his real name was William Henry Morris." Tony said.

I had checked out all of Cosby's books from the library. I grabbed the one called *Fatherhood*.

"Look," I said pointing to a dedication to Bill's father. "I would think it would be noted here if Bill had been adopted."

"You'll see," said Tony. "This whole thing is going to come out. It is really big . . . huge!"

Autumn nodded her head in agreement.

When they headed home in Lois' car, it was Autumn who was driving.

❧

It was only a few weeks after Boris was arrested that a teenage boy named Mikail Markhasev was arrested for killing Cosby's son, Ennis. The media picked up on the uncanny fact that Boris who had given Autumn a ride to the airport and Markhasev were both Russian. Rumors surfaced about the Russian Mafia being involved. The woman who had found Ennis's body was reported to have been involved with a Russian jeweler.

The next time I called Autumn, I asked her, "Do you think Mikail could have been working for Yosie?"

"I don't know. I never heard his name mentioned."

"I see that your mother has done another interview," I told Autumn.

While Cosby was focused on his grief, and Autumn faced prison, Shawn was doing all she could to clear her daughter's name, as well as roll the money in as leaner days were surely ahead. The latest "hot off the press" article was about her time with Cosby in Las Vegas.

"Shawn said in the interview that Cosby wasn't that great of a lover," I told Autumn.

"She only said that because of her present husband, Darrell. My mother has always told me what a great lover Bill was."

Jerold Jackson was also telling his version of the story stating that Cosby was tricked.

Jackson was in prison when Autumn was born. He told the tabloids that Shawn had visited him in prison and confided to him, "Bill is my man now."

He suggested that he had contacted Autumn in the recent past, and that she had confessed to him that she knew he was her father.

When I mentioned that to Autumn, she was furious. "I never told him that," she said, her eyes showing obvious disgust.

"What if Jackson turns out to be your father?" I asked.

"He's not my father!" she exclaimed, repulsed by the very suggestion.

"I'm sure he has some redeeming qualities," I said, trying to reassure her in case he did turn out to be her real father. "And, if he doesn't, there are other relatives, like his mother. I am sure she would be a good person. Maybe you have cousins that would be fun to meet."

"He's not my father!" she repeated fervently. "And I would never have anything to do with him or anyone related to him!"

One day I came home from school to catch the end of a *Geraldo Show* where Shawn was the main guest.

I called Autumn. "Are you watching *Geraldo*?" I asked.

"Yeah, call me back when it's over," she said.

Shawn looked the best she had in years. Her outfit was tasteful and her nails were manicured to perfection—painted in a pale color. Her dark eyes were framed with bangs of jet-black hair and she reminded me of Elizabeth Taylor when she was Shawn's age—a strong spirited woman with conviction, and a force to be reckoned with.

Geraldo wanted to know why Shawn was coming forward.

Shawn explained that no one realized that she and Autumn had a long standing relationship with Cosby.

In Geraldo's no holds barred approach he asked if she had any doubt that her daughter was trying to take money from Bill Cosby.

Shawn then explained that Autumn was homeless and saw selling her story as her only option.

Geraldo interjected that Autumn thought she could blackmail Cosby.

Shawn appeared to be very much in control, yet I supposed that her insides had to be shaking. Mine certainly would have been. Not out of guilt, or not telling the truth, quite the contrary.

It appeared to me that Geraldo was doing everything he could to trip her up. As the segment progressed the strain was starting to show. Her stamina was collapsing. However, she trudged on and let Geraldo know in no uncertain terms that Autumn was Cosby's daughter and that he had been supporting her all these years. She explained that Cosby wouldn't need to do that if he just had slept with someone.

When I called Autumn after the program was over, the first thing she said was, "I thought you were innocent until proven guilty. Geraldo should be sat in a corner wearing one of those white cone hats."

"A dunce cap?"

"Yeah, something like that."

"I can't believe your mother would go on his show to start with. I find Geraldo very intimidating. Maybe it's because he reminds me of an ex-husband I used to have," I told her.

We both laughed.

Autumn added, "My mother isn't intimidated by anyone."

That inner quality of strength was certainly a good one to have at a time like this.

I said, "I don't blame her for walking off the show when she did. It was pretty sly to have Jerold Jackson on a satellite without telling her."

"That's tabloid television," Autumn said. "Bill probably paid Jerold to do it."

During the show Geraldo asked Jerold Jackson if anyone had paid him to say that he was Autumn's dad.

Jackson was adamant that no one had.

⁶⊂⟩⌒⟅₅

More than anyone, Autumn's grandmother Lois was feeling the strain from the burden of caring not only for Autumn, but supporting Tony as well. Was it easy to be generous of spirit? Most of the time, sure, but sometimes, enough was enough and sometimes it was too much, and it felt like the whole thing would never end.

Richard had been the mellowest of all. After Autumn had been released from jail he worked tirelessly to pay for plane tickets, apartments, meals, and even Autumn's fines. Yet he never complained or lost his composure.

Chapter 9

HYSTERICAL PHONE CALLS

We stood outside a restaurant door. It was an early morning hour as we waited for Richard to unlock the car doors.

"Do you have any matches?" Autumn asked, fumbling through her overnight bag in a vain attempt to find some. She wanted to have a puff off a cigar before we continued our 2-hour trip to the Sacramento airport.

When we went to pick Autumn up at her grandmother's, she was still drying clothes and copying tapes for Baum. We helped throw her things in a couple of burgundy nylon bags, and then pulled her out the door. Tony never got up to see her off.

It was the end of May, and we were on our way, once again, to New York for her next court date.

On the plane we discussed her wedding plans—wedding plans that she had only hinted at before. Autumn had an elaborate outline for the auspicious day that she had thought out in great detail.

Certainly planning a wedding would be more appealing than facing the situation she was in, but I had no idea how serious she was about getting married before sentencing. Thinking that her plans were mostly a young woman's fantasy, I listened to them as a dreamy diversion from the fact that we were on our way to another day in court.

"We want to get married on an island off the coast of Florida," Autumn said. "Then we want to take all of the wedding guests on a cruise to Jamaica. Just close family and friends will be invited."

Since we were just daydreaming, I didn't bring up the reality that her bail had an area restriction with a radius of one hundred miles from her grandmother's house. Her day dreams were taking her to a location on the other side of Florida.

"What colors are you going to have?" I asked.

"Gold and cream."

"Oh, gold and ivory will be perfect," I said joining in the fun.

We left the wedding subject and moved on to career ideas. She was no longer into being an architect, but had narrowed her vision to the hotel business. It was an occupation where she had some experience.

"It's always a plus to work at something you want to do before you go into business for yourself," I told her.

"I really love interior design," she said. "I've been watching home improvement programs on television."

"You could open up a Bed & Breakfast rooming house and decorate every room differently," I said, excited at the possibilities. A myriad of designed bedrooms popped into my head. I even made an effort to visualize how Autumn would do them with her interesting concepts of what goes with what, and what is in and what is not. She carried a purse that was dark brown plastic, medium sized, and had a strip of brown and white herringbone print fabric down the front.

"I was lucky to find this at Kmart," she told me, obviously pleased with her purchase.

I would never have looked at it twice, but with her, it worked.

"I was thinking of having a chain of hotels," Autumn added.

"That's even better," I said, impressed with her ability to see a bigger picture. "You'll be able to create all the themes you want. Each hotel could have its own style." I was glad to see she still had ambition toward a profession.

For a time we drifted with our own thoughts. Then Autumn informed me, "*Dateline* wants to get together with me to pitch me for an interview. Robert set it up."

I wondered why she hadn't said something in the car on the way to the airport about the *Dateline* interview. She knew how Richard felt about any of us saying anything to the press. "You don't have to say anything to anyone," I reminded her.

"I know, but I want to. I want to be able to move out of my grandmother's house," she said, thinking there might be a possibility that she would get paid for the interview.

I didn't agree with her thinking but I bit my tongue.

This time we stayed at the *Days Inn* in New Jersey. We checked in, and hung up our clothes. We showed each other what we were going to wear to court.

"I'm going to go outside for a smoke," Autumn said.

"I'll go with you." It made me nervous when she would go off alone to have a smoke, but I had to at least give her that.

We were wound up from the full day of travel. It was dark when we walked out the front door and found a bench to sit on. The temperature was not hot or cold, but just right. However, large quantities of exhaust were wafting up our noses from the busy roadway that ran in front of the hotel. A lot of honking was going on.

The hotel was not as nice as the Marriott we had stayed at before. The paint wasn't fresh, and there wasn't a continental breakfast.

"Autumn it's time to wake up," I told her at 9:30 a.m. The pattern had been much like the previous trip. She was the last one to bed; I was the first one up.

"I have to call Robert," she said, remembering her responsibility. She sleepily punched in his phone number.

"Okay," she said. "We'll be there as soon as we can."

"I thought we were going to have a couple of free days?" I questioned.

"I thought so too, but Robert wants me to get there as soon as I can. He said we have a lot to go over before we go to court again."

We rushed around at a speed that would continue throughout the next seven days.

To catch a bus into Manhattan, we had to maneuver our way through an endless stream of traffic traveling the highway, cross a train overpass, and walk a long-city block on an overgrown, but well-walked dirt path to the Park n' Ride.

Baum took us to lunch and told Autumn, "I contacted the five friends you gave me names for, and none of them will come forward as a character witness. Is there anyone else you can think of?"

"I don't have that many friends," said Autumn. "I spent all that time in Illinois. I was in California and then Florida."

"How about people you went to school with in Illinois?" I ask.

"There wasn't anyone that was close," Autumn said.

Baum brought up Sid, the Pilipino who was working on *Down on the Farm*. "Autumn, he told me there was a part of a letter that was in Yosie's words, and not yours."

"Have you subpoenaed him to be a witness?" I asked Baum.

"No, not yet, I don't want to scare him off."

At the end of the meal Autumn asked for a doggie bag. I was hesitant to start carting leftovers. It had been my experience from the previous trip that they were rarely eaten.

"I hate to waste food," Autumn said. "Especially when so many people go hungry."

"Better to go to waste than to your waist," I told her quoting an old saying.

Baum saw a conflict brewing. "The restaurants will save the food that hasn't been touched, and give it to the homeless including leftover bread. I'm not sure if this is one of those places though," he added, covering his tracks like you would expect a lawyer to do.

Baum let us out of the office at five-o'clock, and I was feeling jet lag setting in.

We did some drugstore shopping, and Autumn told me she wanted to pick up a bottle of vodka.

"I'm too tired to try to find a liquor store Autumn. I want to go home. How about if we just go to the hotel lounge when we get back?"

"Okay, that would be fun," she said, glad there was an alternative to being stuck in the room.

The day had turned out to be hot and humid, and when we returned to our room we dropped off the jackets we hadn't needed, and I peeled off my damp pantyhose. Autumn changed out of her walking shoes, and into some sandals.

The hotel's top floor lounge was heavily air-conditioned which immediately cooled us down. We pulled up stools to the bar, and ordered a round of drinks. We were the only ones there until a man came in and sat down. He started talking to us.

We told him about the long and dangerous walk we had to make that morning to the Park n' Ride. "That highway is treacherous," Autumn said.

I watched you walking across the street this morning," the man said, leaving Autumn and I both feeling uncomfortable.

When the conversation turned to how much trouble we were having finding liquor stores, his demeanor became argumentative.

"Let's get out of here," I told Autumn. "We can take some drinks back to the room."

When we were in the elevator I told Autumn, "That guy was really giving me the creeps when he started talking about watching us out the window."

"Yeah, me too," said Autumn. "He'll be watching us again in the morning. I would bet on it."

We both shuddered.

With two hefty drinks down us and no dinner, we were pretty well floating by the time we crawled into our beds to watch some television.

The phone rang and it was Shawn.

"Let me talk to her," I told Autumn, feeling a rush of sister-in-law friendliness induced by the alcohol.

"I've seen you in the movies," I told Shawn, teasing her.

"I'm in the movies now?" she questioned. "What movies?"

"You know, *Geraldo*," I said, clarifying my incorrect statement.

"I want Autumn to stay with me for the trial," she told me.

"You know how kids are," I said, "They don't want to hang out with their mothers. My daughter doesn't want to hang out with me."

I knew that Autumn didn't want to stay with her mother. However, my effort to find some common ground by sharing children stories, or giving Shawn some reassurance that all mothers faced such rejection, didn't work.

"She's my daughter, and she should be with me," Shawn said forcefully.

I could certainly understand her feelings, but Autumn was growing up and attempting to break ties with her mother as well as Cosby.

"We'll have to leave that up to Autumn and Richard," I said. "They're the ones in charge of those plans. Autumn is an adult now, and can make her own decisions."

"We'll see about that," Shawn said.

I wasn't going to let her have the last word. I started trouble when I told her, "By the way, since you are the only one that has made any money off of this situation, the next time you are making out checks make one out for Autumn so she can buy some clothes for the trial. You haven't even sent her a hundred dollars. Do you think she likes wearing her grandmother's clothes? She also has four impacted wisdom teeth that need to come out!"

"I have three children to look after. If Autumn was living with me, she would have everything she needs." Shawn said in self-defense, knowing darn well that Autumn couldn't live with her if she wanted to. It would have been in violation of her bail.

When Shawn was done talking, she told me to put Autumn on the phone.

She told Autumn, "Jewel says that I'm a bad mother."

Autumn had been sitting right there the whole time I was talking to Shawn, and she knew I hadn't said any such thing.

I had really stirred the pot though. I couldn't hear what Shawn was saying, but I could hear her yelling. Autumn had to hold the phone away from her ear. Finally, she told her mother, "I'm sorry I messed things up for you. I have already told you that." After a good half hour of listening to her mother Autumn reached a point of numbness and hung up the phone without saying a word.

Autumn said, "I need to call my grandmother before my mom does." She called Lois and let out a wail like a wounded animal. The tears poured out of her eyes as she described the injustice her mother had just committed—upsetting her when what she needed was peace and quiet. She knew exactly how to get Lois's sympathy, and she was right. The rigors of being in so much trouble was unbelievably stressful for those of us who were around her. To be her would have been unbearable. She was like her uncle though in keeping her composure, and she complained very little for being in her situation.

"I will talk to Shawn," Lois promised.

Autumn stayed up until late into the night venting her frustration over her mother's disturbing phone call.

"I'm tired of my mother's abuse," Autumn said.

"What do you mean?" I asked. "Has she hit you?"

"No, nothing like that. She would just go off and leave me with my brother and sisters and I never knew if she was coming back. One time she left for a whole month."

"That must have been awful," I responded, "and scary."

"It was."

"It must have also been hard to have Bill be America's Father for everyone but you," I added.

"It really was. I would watch Fat Albert on television and think that is my father's voice. I can't tell you what that felt like. I wanted to meet him and get to know him. Grandma was the one who set it up so that I could meet him."

"What was that like?" I asked.

"It was great. He was really funny and he gave me a stuffed bear," Autumn beamed, and then her mood turned solemn. She became quiet while trying to sort her feelings.

I could sense a chrysalis shedding its cocoon and a butterfly ready to ascend. It was a process, and Autumn was doing her best to work through it—to shed the skin that had been holding her back from the woman she was destined to become.

I could see how growing up without a father was one thing, but to grow up without a mother being present meant that Autumn was raising herself. Mistakes are a lot easier to make when you don't have someone there to guide you. Parents who are missing in action, even if it's just emotionally, leaves you with no one to trust or go to for guidance. Was it any wonder Autumn had turned to Yosie when he showed her fatherly attention?

I studied Autumn in the darkened room. She sat on the edge of her bed framed in a blue-white light that was reflecting harshly off the side of the building across the way.

"You don't have to stay with me, when you go to trial," I told her. "It is up to you and Richard, just like I told your mother."

"I know," said Autumn. "I don't want to stay with my mother."

Again, I made her a promise. "We'll do whatever it takes to get you through this, and to the trial."

The next time we went to Baum's office, he and Autumn talked privately, and I started the search for an apartment for us to stay in during the trial. Baum had let us know that it would take the month of July to get through all of the court proceedings.

"Here is a *Village Voice* paper," he said, sitting me down at his desk. "You should find some good leads in the classifieds."

When he left the room, I started my calls. In between dialing phone numbers, I looked at the picture of his wife, and glanced at some of the messages on his desk. They were all concerning Autumn.

Chapter 10

RAIN IN WHITE PLAINS

Our next trip to New York was in the beginning of June. Autumn started work on her defense for her trial that had been scheduled to start in July. I could hear Autumn's laughter ringing loudly—echoing through the conference room. It couldn't be all work that they were doing; Baum and Autumn were having too much fun.

Baum exhibited a definite father-like affection toward Autumn. I could see that he truly adored her. She was relaxed with him, and counted on him to save her from her self-inflicted destiny.

When Baum and Autumn broke for lunch we walked to a Chinese restaurant in Chinatown. I waited until Autumn went to the restroom to talk to Baum about Tony. "I don't want Tony to stay with us during the trail," I told Baum. "It will be hard enough just being two women living together. I don't want to be a third wheel the way Lois has been."

"It will be better if he doesn't stay with you," he said. "The prosecution has plenty of money and they will put him up in a hotel if they have to."

When Autumn returned to the table I told her what we had been talking about. "It will be better if Tony doesn't stay with us during the trial since he is on the prosecution's side."

"I can understand that," Autumn said.

"The media would have a field day, and it wouldn't look good," Baum added.

After lunch, *NBC* sent a car to pick us up so that *Dateline* could make their pitch for an interview. Though Richard had insisted we all keep quiet and not do any interviews, Baum insisted we had to at least give these folks a chance to talk to Autumn for his sake, if nothing else.

I liked Baum a lot, and I knew he was doing everything in his power to vindicate Autumn. He had been good about handling the *Hard Copy* pitch, so I agreed that it would be okay.

I was expecting a limousine, but a black Lincoln Town Car showed up instead. When we arrived at a large Fifth Avenue skyscraper, we were greeted by Wendy Sachs, an associate producer for *Dateline*.

We were ushered past security to the floor where *Dateline* conducts its business. We entered a corner office with an oval conference table and chairs. At the center of the table was a basket of juices and spring water. The windows offered a view of Fifth Avenue.

Wendy introduced us to another producer and then to Ed Gordon, the show's host who would be asking Autumn questions.

"*Dateline* has four times the viewing of other television tabloids," Gordon told us.

Baum brought up the video that Lois had made of Autumn with Cosby when she met him as a teenager. "Perhaps you could use that," Baum offered.

"Who is selling whom?" I asked.

Everyone laughed.

Ed directed his next statement to Autumn, "I would say to you that this is not an easy thing. I can promise you, I will be fair to you."

"What do you want to see happen, Autumn?" someone asked.

"I want to be able to tell my side of the story," Autumn answered.

When Cosby's name came up, Ed said, "He'll make a call, I'm sure."

"Will Autumn get to know the questions you're going to ask her?" I asked.

I received an emphatic, "No!"

"Autumn, you're not going to like all the questions," Ed explained. "I'll have to ask some hard ones. But, you want believability!"

"Will Autumn get paid?" I asked, knowing that she was hoping she would.

"We don't pay for our interviews," the producer said, almost apologetically.

Back on the street, there was a long line of black Town Cars under the employ of *NBC*. We were directed to the one that would be giving us a ride back to Baum's office.

We went back a different way than we had come. We passed by back-street barrios, and an old hospital that had a playground next door. Standing guard was a twelve-foot plaster and stained glass mosaic dragon.

"I love the art in New York," I commented. "It shows up in the most interesting places. Look at that dragon Autumn."

"Oh yeah," she said when I pulled her from her personal thoughts. After viewing the artwork she quickly drifted back into silence.

After we left Baum's office for the day, we followed phone-book directions to a liquor store. Autumn purchased some citrus flavored vodka, and then we headed to our New Jersey hotel. After mixing drinks we ordered Italian in, and shared some tiramisu dessert.

The next day was a play day of sorts. Baum took us apartment hunting in preparation for the upcoming trial. He said he would take us by a local college to post a want ad for a room. Before going there, I insisted Baum show us an apartment I had found in the paper.

"I've lived here all my life," Baum said. "I don't think you're going to like the neighborhood."

The apartment I had called about was in Greenwich Village, and I wanted to see the infamous area. "Okay," I said, but I want to check it out anyway. At least I will feel like we are eliminating possibilities."

Slovenly dressed people started to dominate the streets as we approached the appointed address.

"Look at that guy," said Autumn. "He wouldn't think much about hitting one of us over the head!"

A bearded man dressed in bright orange bell-bottom pants shuffled past. It looked like it had been a long time since he had a smile on his face.

"You're right," I told Baum, when we saw less than I had hoped for. It had looked promising in the paper, but only a block or two off the main street landed us in a ghetto.

"It might be okay here if we didn't have to be dressed up for court every day," I said, a little discouraged.

Autumn sat in the back seat enjoying a bit of solitude while Baum drove to a college where we could check bulletin boards for summer rentals.

"You'll love Brooklyn. Let's go there," Baum said. "I know a great place to have lunch."

"Yeah, that sounds good," Autumn said perking up. "We never had breakfast."

Autumn rarely had breakfast, but it was getting close to lunch.

"Yes, I'm starting to feel a bit hollow," I joined in.

We checked with some real estate agents in a "hip" part of Brooklyn. I almost wished Autumn wasn't with me for fear that we might be discriminated against. I could only imagine what people were thinking of us: a middle-aged white woman looking for an apartment with a young black woman.

"I have a room that might come up for rent in a big house," one agent offered.

I eagerly gave him my number as the first positive step toward renting a place.

Robert knew all the best restaurants. He took us to an artsy, modern-type corner building. Inside, the pastel painted walls were covered with a local artist's work.

"I love the colors, "I told Autumn.

"They're really nice," she agreed as she looked around.

A few people looked up from their plates, seeing Autumn as a familiar face. But so far on this trip the press hadn't been present, and the recognition was coming harder than when her face had been plastered on the headline news every day.

"You know what I would do?" She thought for a moment and then gave her view from the point of an aspiring interior designer—her latest career quest. "I would put glass in the dividers at the back of the booths."

Her taste was eclectic, and hard to second guess, but sometimes we did find mutual ground to agree upon.

"Stained glass would be fun," I added.

After lunch we walked through some of the cute shops in the neighborhood, and then went back to Baum's office so that he and Autumn could work some more on the case. There were three large boxes of files and the trial hadn't even started. Baum wanted to go over everything in them.

I sat in his office and looked at some magazines I had just purchased. No one else was in the building on the weekend, so there were just the three of us.

Baum's personal phone line rang.

"Can you answer that, Jewel?" he yelled from the other room.

It was his wife.

"Who is this?" she asked.

"This is Jewel, Autumn's aunt," I told her.

"Where's Robert?"

"He's walking in the door, hold on."

Robert took the phone and Autumn stuck her head in the room, saying, "Jewel, put your clothes back on!"

She was joking of course, but I was hoping that Baum's wife hadn't heard the comment. "Hey," I said. "Are you trying to get me in trouble?"

Autumn was smiling at me with a devilish grin.

Autumn didn't have much to be laughing about, and it was good to see she still had her delightful, or in this case, mischievous sense of humor.

When Baum and Autumn were finished with the paper work, Baum dropped us off in the ritzy So Ho area of Manhattan. We had dinner at an outdoor restaurant.

"Look!" exclaimed Autumn.

There was an old man riding a bicycle with an old radio strapped to the back fender. It was blasting out Frank Sinatra's rendition of *New York*.

"Come on," I told Autumn. "It's time to get to the theater."

Richard had said we could have a night on the town, and I picked a modern dance to take Autumn to at the off-Broadway Joyce Theater.

"I've never seen modern dancing before," she said.

The performance was superb, and she heartily joined in the zealous clapping at the end.

When we left the theater it was dark, but the streets were still crowded. However the subway wasn't, and it felt unnerving to be the only ones waiting for a train late at night.

"There goes a rat," Autumn said, as we waited for a light coming from the tunnel.

A small rat scurried over the tracks below, darting in and out of the trash.

When we boarded the train there was only one guy in the car. He was rough looking and he moved from where he was sitting to come and sit across from us.

I was worried he was going to try to rob us, so I gave him my most severe look and never took my eyes off of him, while Autumn did her best to look away from him. After about a minute of staring him down he moved to another car, to our great relief. I vowed we would never ride the trains that late at night again.

Baum gave us the next day off, and we never left the hotel room. I read the New York Times Sunday paper, which was as thick as a book.

Autumn set about foot-washing a load of clothes in the bathtub. She took a lot of cigar-smoking breaks.

We watched a comedy on television, and ordered Chinese delivery.

Tony called, and Autumn laughed a lot.

"I found the best watermelon juice," she told him. She was silent while he was speaking and then said, "Okay, I love you."

When she hung up she told me, "Tony didn't want to talk anymore if all we have to talk about is juice."

Monday was court day, and when I got up and looked out the window, it was raining. It had been hot and muggy all week, but this was the first day it had rained.

"Autumn, it's raining," I told her when I woke her up.

"Is it?" she asked, sounding a bit discouraged.

We didn't have to be at Baum's until noon, and I had found an apartment for us to go and look at. We dressed in our court clothes and headed out with our umbrellas.

Autumn usually wore tennis shoes back and forth to Baum's office, but she had put on her good court shoes.

"My feet are soaked," Autumn complained after we had walked many blocks, in the wrong direction.

"Why didn't you wear your other shoes?" I asked.

"I don't know. I just got dressed for court."

We ran out of time, and had to go to Baum's office without seeing the elusive apartment.

Baum rushed us out for a quick lunch before heading to Grand Central Station to catch a train to White Plains. We boarded the train with just a few minutes to spare. Cosby's attorney was sitting in the first seat of the train car we entered. I think we'll try another car," Baum said, turning an about face.

The attorneys of Yosie and Boris were in the next train car. Baum sat with them, and Autumn and I sat in the seat behind them. I tried to listen to what they were discussing while Autumn rode along with her eyes closed.

I overheard Yosie's lawyer say, "Every time I turn around, Cosby is on television."

I had noticed the same thing and had commented as much to Autumn. "Cosby must have a great public relations agent," I told her. "He even did a *Touched by an Angel* episode where they had him act the part of an angel. Someone is going all out to make sure he looks like a saint."

When I had mentioned the same thing to Richard, he joked, "He probably isn't getting much attention from his wife after everything coming out about his affair. He has to do something."

The rain continued to pour down, and we took a cab from the train station to the modern style courthouse in White Plains.

Even after using our umbrellas we were damp through to our skin. In the courtroom the air conditioning was going full blast and it chilled us to the bone.

Another case was ahead of Autumn's. A woman lawyer, who was

pacing back and forth in front of an angled podium, was questioning a policeman. She asked him the same questions over and over, and even the judge became bored with her strategy.

"Can we move on?" the judge asked.

It was the first time we had seen the woman judge who would ultimately decide Autumn's fate.

The judge looked like she could be Martha Stewart's cousin. She had short blonde hair and her bangs fell near one eye like Martha's. She was round faced and void of any visible makeup.

I looked at Autumn, realizing how serious the situation was. She looked back, expressionless, but knowing full well why I was looking at her.

Autumn was called before the judge.

"The United States against Autumn Jackson!" the bailiff sang out.

Baum requested a subpoena for a net-worth statement on Cosby's wealth. The purpose was to show the relevance between what he was worth and the fraction of that amount Autumn had asked for in exchange for her life story.

"After reviewing all the papers, I won't agree to a subpoena for the details to the net-worth," Judge Jones said.

Boris's lawyer, Anthony Cueto, argued for a severance motion to separate Boris's trial from the others because he felt there would be a spillover effect against Boris, limiting him to a fair trial.

Judge Jones denied the motion.

Yosie's lawyer, Neil Checkman requested a bail reform since Yosie hadn't been able to meet the bail requirements that were the same as Autumn's—two hundred and fifty thousand dollars.

"I'm not going to overturn Judge Peck's decision," Judge Jones said.

We left the courthouse and headed back to the train. It was still raining in torrents.

It fit the results of the day. Everything asked for had been turned down.

Realizing Judge Jones wasn't going to be easily moved, Autumn was disheartened. The gloom of the rain fit her looming fate.

Chapter 11

FIREWORKS

"Hi, Pokey, it's me, JJ! Are you there?" I shouted into the answering machine at the other end of the phone.

It was 2:00 p.m. It was the end of June and the California sunshine was intense. The heat in Clearlake was breaking 100 degrees. I assumed that Autumn would be up and getting ready for the next day's trip to New York. This time we were going for the trial. The months of waiting and wondering what her fate would be were finally coming to an end.

"Ola," a sleepy voice answered at the other end.

"Are you ready to go?" I asked enthusiastically.

"What flight are we on?" she asked.

"We're taking Continental this time," I told her. We had used a different airline every time. It was always left up to me to make the arrangements. Autumn had never concerned herself with the details as she had enough to think about.

"What time are we leaving?"

"We'll pick you up at 6 a.m." I answered. "Do you have your clothes ready for court?"

"I didn't have a chance to do any sewing," she said. "I'll get a credit card from grandma, and shop in New York."

"Is Tony going to come with us in the morning?" I asked.

"Yeah, he's planning on it."

"Don't forget your identification," I reminded her. "You can't get on the plane without it."

"I know."

"We need to bring a flashlight. The landlady said she'll leave a key under some garbage in the entry way if she has to leave before we get there," I told her.

"Under some garbage?" she asked.

"That's what she told me."

It had been a challenge to rent a place sight unseen, but that is what it had come to. I contacted an agency that was able to find us a place in Greenwich Village. Baum told me it was an okay neighborhood, but it was hard not to be leery of what the conditions would be. Our flight didn't arrive until well after dark, and the thought of thrashing through a pile of trash to find an ominous key left me with an uneasy feeling.

§☾✿☽§

The next morning, at 8:15 a.m., Autumn and I kissed our guys goodbye as we made ready to board the plane. We wouldn't see them for a whole month. Tony wouldn't be coming to New York unless he had to testify. Richard would stay behind to do what he did best, work and send money for the costly trip.

Once on the plane, I was able to catch up with what had been happening with Autumn.

"I would never get an abortion," Autumn confided.

"You aren't pregnant, are you?" I asked, hoping that she would say "no." Even though I knew that was not the best way to ask a question, I was hoping for a positive answer.

"I might be," she said. "I'm a few days late."

"For your sake, I hope that you're not. If you have to go to prison you would have to give up the baby, and that would be worse than anything you could imagine."

"Tony will take care of it."

"But you're the one who'd be missing it. You're facing a minimum of five years, and Baum said it doesn't look good. Believe me; having a baby would only make things harder on you."

"But Tony would have a part of me," she countered.

"You don't want to miss your baby growing up," I argued. "The child would be five years old by the time you got out. Having a baby is something you and Tony should enjoy together."

"That would be ideal, but I might already be pregnant."

"Let's pray that you're not."

§☾✿☽§

Autumn and I were starting to learn the ways of New York City. When we landed, a pre-hired limousine driver greeted us.

It was hot and muggy outside much like it had been on the previous visit and the warm air assaulted our air-conditioned faces.

The limo had seen better days, but we were glad to climb into the comfort of the stretch, and slide across the large leather seats. The limousine slowly rolled into Manhattan.

We had been on the road since early morning and exhaustion was setting in.

The passenger car was set up in a traditional style, but the crystal containers that should have held liquor were empty.

"I've never been in a limousine before," Autumn said with the excitement of a child.

"Let's celebrate that," I said, producing a small bottle of homemade coffee liqueur from my overnight bag.

The only light was from oncoming cars, and in their harsh glare, I could see her face beaming.

I poured the dark liquid into crystal glasses that were in a wooden holder on the door.

"Here's to your first limo ride," I said, holding up my glass to click with hers. "Salute!"

"Cheers!" Autumn reciprocated.

It was over an hour's ride to the apartment we had rented. The Fourth of July weekend traffic made driving tedious, and we pulled up more than an hour after I told the landlady that we would be arriving.

I was relieved to see her face peering out the front-door window as we cruised to a stop.

"You're on the fourth floor," Linda said, after introducing herself as the keeper of the ancient apartment building.

The stairs were old, rickety, and filthy. Linda helped hoist our luggage up the four flights. There wasn't any elevator. Our apartment was the last one on the last floor.

Linda wore a long hippie skirt, and her hair was two-toned—months past needing a touch-up.

We entered a quaint apartment, fixed up with a few old pieces of furniture. A wood hutch encasing the kitchenette sink and cabinets was the highlight of the apartment. The window-mounted air-conditioner was turned on, and the apartment was bordering on cool.

"This is my niece, Autumn," I said, once we had finished the couple of trips up and down the stairs, and were finally catching our breath.

If she had any question as to the difference in color between Autumn and me, she didn't say anything.

"The apartment is really cute," I added with relief. My fears were finally abated. We would be comfortable there.

After I signed the necessary papers, and gave Linda the balance of cashier's checks needed for the rent, she left.

Autumn busied herself checking out the details of the one-bedroom suite. "I'll take this side of the closet," she said as she unpacked the clothes that needed hanging. "I'm going out for a smoke," she said when she was finished.

"Stay at the bottom of the stairs," I said with warning. Though I wasn't supposed to let her out of my sight, I knew I would have to at least offer her the freedom to sit on the stoop in peace, and by herself.

I would have the bedroom, and she would have a bed in the living room with access to the television which she enjoyed watching much more than I did.

We were too wound up to sleep, so we ventured out into the neighborhood even though it was 11:00 p.m.

There were a lot of people out strolling about, and we joined in.

We found a deli not far from the apartment, and stocked up on a few supplies. There was a watermelon that looked delightful.

"How much is this watermelon?" Autumn asked the store vendor.

"One dollar," he said in broken English.

"This watermelon is only a dollar," Autumn said, pleased at the opportunity for a bonus purchase.

It turned out to be a dollar per pound and we ended up paying sixteen dollars for the melon.

"That deli won't get another dollar from us," Autumn promised, upset that the clerk hadn't made the price clear.

We went back to the apartment to unpack our purchases, and called everyone to let them know we had arrived.

"I can't hear you," Richard said.

The phone had a bad connection, and it was hard to hear anything.

"Get that fixed first thing in the morning," he yelled seemingly across the country.

Though sleep had been fitful, the morning was glorious. We had windows that opened to the street, and we were at the height of the treetops. We could hear the birds singing, and we could watch them fly and land on the branches.

The balmy weather felt almost tropical, and people were out in full regalia by the time I woke up Autumn.

She called Baum at 9:30, but he was held up. He was busy finishing another case.

"I'll call you later," he told her. "I want you to take a lie detector test. The *Globe* is saying you refused to take one."

"It was Yosie who refused," she clarified.

We were the first tenants who had rented the apartment on a monthly basis. It was under-stocked, and we made a list of things we would need to make it functional.

"We need an extra set of keys," Autumn said. She needed to be able to come and go out the front security door to smoke her cigars.

"I need a fan for my bedroom," I told her. "And, we need to do some real grocery shopping so we don't have to eat all of our meals in restaurants."

We went out to the street that had a steady flow of foot traffic. Cars and taxies honked their horns in a constant rhythm of impatience.

"I love this," I told Autumn. "It's so fun to set up an apartment with a girlfriend. I feel like I just graduated high school."

She looked at me and smiled. For her it wasn't fun. We were there because she was in trouble and that stayed foremost on her mind.

When we walked into a hardware store to have the extra keys made she saw the man who played the character of Cousin Larry, in the sitcom *Perfect Strangers*.

Autumn walked up to him and told him, "I really liked your show."

When she came back by me, I told her, "You should ask him for his autograph, and then give him yours."

The shopkeeper was listening to what I said, but he didn't get the humor. In a couple of days Autumn's face would be on the front page of every New York newspaper, and then he would get the joke.

When we returned home the phone was ringing and Autumn answered the phone hoping it was Tony. Her expression completely changed when she realized it was her mother.

"Okay," Autumn said. "We'll see you when you get here."

"She wants to talk to you," Autumn said, holding out the phone.

"How's everything going?" Shawn asked. "I bought Autumn a few things that I'll bring with me. I'll be there soon. I'm on my way over."

One thing about family. You can't hold a grudge. For Autumn's sake, I had to forget about our last uncomfortable phone call. I could understand Shawn wanting to see where we would be staying. She would have liked nothing more than to take my place and be the one rooming with her daughter. If Autumn had been my daughter I would have wanted to stay with her too. A parent's instinct to protect their child is built in. Shawn may have wanted to protect Autumn, but it was too late.

Autumn was doing her best to keep her mother at arm's length.

It's never easy to have your child go through a phase of shunning you to attain their independence. It hurts, and you wonder why it has to be that way. None-the-less, during all the chaos surrounding court that was exactly what was happening between Autumn and Shawn.

Nothing makes you grow up faster than diversity and Autumn was smack in the middle of a national scandal. She may have entered the arena a fledgling adult, but that was changing quickly.

९८)৲১₰

During a trip out to have a smoke, Autumn tried the trap door to the roof. The next-door neighbor caught her.

"You'd better not let the landlady catch you up there," she said. "I've lived here a long time and been through three landlords. This one closed off the garden we used to be able to sit in, and she doesn't want us on the roof."

"I thought it would be a good place for a smoke," Autumn told her as she climbed back down a rod-iron ladder.

"I'll tell you what," the neighbor said, "why don't you join me up there to watch the fireworks tonight. I was going to sneak up there. I have watched them from up there for nearly 30 years."

When nighttime came we went up with the neighbor. The roof was unsteady and sagging. I was afraid we might fall through. I was glad Autumn had been discouraged from smoking up there. It would have been a real fire hazard. Still, it was fun to watch the fireworks display going off at Stanton Island, and listen to the stories the aged woman had to tell.

"An old woman dropped dead in your apartment," she told us. "That was when Linda decided to create the monthly rental."

Autumn and I looked at each other and wondered if we would be dealing with a ghost.

"The fireworks were fun," I told Autumn after we climbed back down through the hatched door.

"Yeah, it was," Autumn said, and she thanked the neighbor woman for inviting us.

"My period started," Autumn told me, when we were getting ready for bed.

I breathed a deep sigh of relief.

The next day Tony called Autumn and told her he had a big fight with Lois.

Autumn over-reacted to the information, and was irate at Lois. "I can't believe my grandmother," she cried. "She's supposed to be supporting me, and fighting with Tony isn't the way to do it."

She called her grandmother and yelled at her, "Tony wasn't doing anything wrong!"

"I want Tony out of here," Lois told her

When they hung up I told Autumn, "This has been hard on everyone. I'm sure your grandmother is ready to have her home back to herself."

"Look how tough this is on me!" Autumn cried. "I'm the one facing prison. I don't need this aggravation."

The more she talked about it, the more tears there were streaming down her face. She started to hiccup over being so upset. "Tony didn't do anything wrong," she said, trying to convince me as well. "Grandma thought he was fooling around with one of our friends, but he would never do that."

"How do you know?" I asked, marveling at her faith in him.

"He wouldn't do that while I'm here going to trial."

I certainly hoped that was the case. I let her carry on for over a half-hour knowing that she probably needed the release. She had been really brave through most of the ordeal and she had to feel much more frustration than everyone else. Her face was red and swollen from her tears.

Finally, I said, "Let's go for a walk."

The fresh air helped to calm her, and soon we were having fun looking around the little neighborhood shops. We stopped in at a corner bar, and found out that the poet Dylan Thomas had hung out there. It was called the *White Horse Tavern*, and it was on the city's walking scenic-tour map. The ceiling was lined with embossed tin plating. Many spilt beers had soaked into the wooden floor giving it a permanent aroma of hops and alcohol. It was cool inside, giving relief from the mid-summer heat and humidity.

One of the waiters recognized Autumn.

"Do you know who that is?" he asked a couple of his friends who were also escaping the heat and drinking a couple of beers.

Overhearing his question, I said, "We're just trying to relax. Tell them who she is after we leave."

"Got ya," he said, smiling with his secret knowledge.

Back at the apartment, we put away our food and other goods. We rested for a couple of hours and then dressed to go out to dinner.

Right across from the *White Horse Tavern* we found a delightful Italian restaurant. Tables were set up outside with umbrellas overhead. It was a little too warm to be hanging around outside, and we were instantly perspiring for doing so, but it was fun to watch the people walking by. We endured the humid heat, and enjoyed a few minutes of not having to think about the real reason we were in New York—Autumn's trial.

Chapter 12

LIE DETECTOR TEST

"Come over here!" a street musician shouted to Autumn. "I'll play you a song."

"Should I go over there?" she asked me.

"I guess it would be all right," I answered, and we crossed the street to get closer to the live music.

Two African American men were playing guitars. Their sound was only mediocre, but they were having a good time.

"Is that a cigar you're smoking?" the man who had done the shouting asked Autumn.

She nodded her head affirmatively, flattered that he had asked.

"That's fine, as long as you don't have a deep voice," he joked.

"What song do you want to hear?" he asked, and then teased, "Let me hear your baritone!"

Autumn laughed, and named a couple of numbers he wasn't familiar with.

"I'll play this for you," he said, picking out a tune his partner and he played with regularity.

When they were finished, Autumn and I each tossed a dollar into the top hat they had laid out for tips.

We started to leave when he asked us to stay for one more song.

"Are you the one on TV?" he asked Autumn.

"That's it! We're out of here," I said, pulling her along. "The next thing you know he'll be asking you for a date."

"I would have told him I was married," she said, allowing herself to be led like an obedient child.

"You're not married yet."

"I will be."

We looked back to see a New York cop chasing the singing duo off the sidewalk.

Another woman stopped us on the street as we headed home. I started to press Autumn behind me, but she said it was okay. The woman took Autumn's hand and told her, "I hope you get the money from Cosby!"

Autumn had become less fearful of these chance encounters and reacted with poise and grace. She would patiently listen to people who had no idea of what was really happening. There was no money to be had. She would thank them for their concern, never making an attempt to explain how things really where. In reality, she was fighting to stay out of prison.

In the middle of the night Autumn came into my room. "Are you awake?" she asked.

"I am now," I told her.

"I'm itching all over," she said. "Look!"

"Come into the bathroom," I directed, and then searched for my glasses.

Under a bright light, I could see a distinct rash covering Autumn's neck and face.

"Look here," she said lifting her sleep shirt. "I have bumps on my stomach and under my arms."

"It looks like hives," I said. "You did get awfully upset about the fight between your grandmother and Tony. This could be a reaction."

"I did cry a lot," she agreed. "What should I do?"

"I'm not sure. How about taking a cool bath?"

"I already tried that."

"I have a sleeping pill you can take. They aren't very strong, and maybe if you get a good night's sleep the rash will disappear."

However, by morning the welts were spreading, and were larger.

"Do you think we need to go to the hospital?" I asked her.

Autumn wasn't one to complain, but she was visibly suffering. "I don't know what to do," she said in desperation.

We hurriedly dressed and went to a pharmacy. She bought some anti-itch cream, which she started using immediately.

She took the remainder with her as we headed toward Lower Manhattan.

"Are you nervous about the lie detector test?" I asked.

"A little."

"I would be too," I said, trying to share her feelings.

We quickly walked the six blocks to the subway at 14th Street. We walked another two blocks once we were underground. It took riding two trains and another mile of walking to get to Baum's office.

The lie detector test took place in one of the top-story offices of the Legal Aid Department. The test didn't take long; no more than an hour.

We were on the way home when I asked her, "How did you do?"

"I passed the test with 99.96% accuracy," she bragged.

"What does that mean?"

"That's as good as you can get," she grinned.

"What else happened? What were you asked?"

"The man doing the test put straps around my chest. He asked me if I believed Mr. Cosby was my father in several different ways."

"What did you tell him?"

"I told him Mr. Cosby is my father," she said, reconfirming her belief.

The next day we had to be in court. The jurors were to be selected. When we arrived at Baum's office, Shawn was there.

We crossed the street to the courthouse. My spot at Autumn's side was preempted by her mother. I walked to the far side of Shawn, and sometimes dropped in behind Autumn. The press carried on the same pomp and circumstance as usual.

Picking the jury was a long and laborious project. Judge Jones sat to the side of her bench hunched over. It looked like she was strained under the weight of her heavy black judge's robe.

The lawyers, and the candidates to be the summoned rulers of Autumn's destiny, huddled in front of the judge. "Do you regularly watch the Cosby Show?" she asked. It was assumed most everyone knew who Cosby was, so they didn't try to find jurors who didn't know of him, but instead were impartial to him.

Not only had everyone heard of him, most of them were great fans.

The time went by slowly as person after person was eliminated. One of the released was a woman who was so pregnant she had to hold her belly up. She gladly waddled away.

A woman sitting in front of me had a wretched sounding cough, and she turned around to ask me for a Kleenex.

Shawn was restless and decided to go to the store. I didn't want her to go alone. There would still be a crowd of reporters outside. I talked her into using the side-entrance to avoid the press. But on the way back, she brazenly walked up the front stairs of the courthouse. She had been Cosby's lover, and she was Autumn's mother. I don't think she felt the need to sneak around.

"We'll try a different approach tomorrow," Shawn said, sensing my attempt to minimize attention.

"Once the trial starts, I'm going to be staying in the courtroom with Autumn," I told her. "I won't be leaving to go anywhere."

We ran into Wendy Sachs from *Dateline*, and Shawn said, "Autumn and Jewel are living on 11th Street in Greenwich Village.

Wendy watched my mouth drop. Keeping our whereabouts from the press was paramount.

When we were alone, I told Shawn emphatically, "Don't tell anyone where we live!"

Over a hundred people were interviewed for the position of juror. I couldn't hear the answers they were giving the judge, but at the end, each of the finalists was asked about their background. A woman who has been selected kept getting up to shake out her legs that had fallen asleep. She was released. One man kept nodding off, his head jerking violently as he succumbed to slumber. He was also released. The lawyers were then given a chance to eliminate a couple more of the selection.

Baum wasn't completely pleased with the final grouping, but he couldn't do anymore to change it. There was one woman left on the jury who was a lawyer of some type. She seemed very together, and we all hoped she would have sympathy for Autumn.

During breaks, Autumn would run to the bathroom and apply more of her anti-itch cream. "It's really hard to sit still," she said. "The inside of my thighs are the worst, and since they touch they are really itching."

Autumn had been positioned at the front of the courtroom, and everyone was sure to look at her as they walked up to the judge, and again when they walked away. She was doing her best not to move at all, and she sat rigid while facing forward. I would have been squirming like mad with that rash, but she sat amazingly still, and no one was the wiser.

At the end of the day, we made our procession back to Baum's office. Shawn had a bag of casual clothes with her, and was ready to come back to our apartment. "I'm going to go home with you," she informed us.

We took a cab, and she told us about someone named Wanda Akin whom she wanted us to meet.

"Who is she?" Autumn asked.

"A friend of mine," Shawn said. "She has a really nice apartment."

Autumn asked a couple more questions, and soon found out that this supposed friend was looking to sign Autumn up for a book.

"I don't think we'll be going over there," I told Shawn, to Autumn's relief.

The three of us went to the Italian restaurant across from the *White Horse Tavern*.

After dinner Shawn suggested, "I can stay with you tonight."

That wasn't going to happen, and I was sure to let her know it. "No Shawn, you have your own place to stay." It was my job to make sure that Autumn had as much rest as possible. Plus there was nowhere for Shawn to sleep. The morning would have been a disaster with us all trying to get into the bathroom at once to hurry back to the courthouse. Shawn hailed a taxi.

After we saw her off, Autumn and I went upstairs and dressed for bed. It had been a long day. Autumn had gone through two tubes of cortisone cream, and sat down on her spongy couch bed to apply another layer of the lotion.

"I wrote a bedtime story," I told her.

"A bedtime story?" she questioned.

"Yes, but not the Cinderella kind. This is a romantic bedtime story that has some people, places, and things we have experienced in New York. Do you want to hear it?"

"Sure," she said. She curled up, getting comfortable against a stack of pillows. I sat in an antique overstuffed chair next to a floor lamp. Our living room was made charming by the age and character of the apartment, and the small size lent itself well to bedtime reading.

"The story is called, The Smell of Gardenias," I said, and I started to read. One of the main characters was fashioned after the neighbor with whom we had watched the fireworks.

The next morning Autumn went downstairs to have a smoke. She heard some noise outside the front door. Peeking out the soiled window, she could see two guys having sex. She backed up and sat on the stairs until they were finished and gone. "They left the wrapper to a condom on the steps," she said with the voice of a child.

"Well, at least they practiced safe sex," I said, trying to make light of the shady event.

When we returned home from court that night, it didn't take long to realize that the landlady had been in our apartment. We had left official papers on Autumn's trial sitting on the table. We had called in a list of needs to her, but she hadn't addressed those. Instead, she had taken out our garbage!

I called Linda and told her I wanted to know beforehand if she was going to be in the apartment. "Emptying our garbage isn't something we expect you to do," I told her. "But, we do need you to get us another phone and another set of keys."

Again, Shawn came home with us. We went to *Caliente's* for dinner. It was a very happening Mexican restaurant with a margarita happy hour.

Shawn was drinking shots of Jose Cuervo as chasers to her margaritas.

"I hardly ever drink anymore," she was telling us as she downed another full shot of tequila.

I knew what she was talking about. The whole situation was very high energy and very explosive. We were all indulging in abnormal behavior. We were all trying to control the impossible. It was like trying to pull a flying car out of a tornado. It couldn't be done. Most of the time we felt like we were spinning around in the tornado itself, being flung from one side to the other.

A couple of hours later, Autumn put Shawn into a cab and we headed home.

Richard called just before we went to bed, and he told Autumn what to do about her hives. The next day we went to the store and bought her some pills which started to work almost instantly.

Richard had also told me, "Booby trap the front door so you know when the landlady is coming in and out. Put a matchbook in the door, and if it's been moved while you're gone you will know someone has been in your place."

"I wrote another bedtime story while you were working with Baum," I told Autumn. "This one is about the two guys you saw in the doorway."

After I read the fictional rendition of her earlier observation, she told me, "Your story is better than the real life version."

Reading the quickly written bedtime stories would become an anticipated event, giving Autumn a temporary release from the dire reality of the day.

Chapter 13

THE GAMES BEGIN

"Get up Autumn," I said for the second time. "Today is the first day of your trial."

"Okay," she said, straining to open her eyes.

Neither one of us had slept more than a few restless hours.

Baum was pacing the floor when we arrived. He was ready to make our strut to the courthouse.

Autumn needed to change from her walking shoes into her courtroom shoes. She was in the restroom struggling to get into her pale white pantyhose. "Everyone is ready to go," I told her.

Lois had been subpoenaed to the trial as a possible witness. She was kneeling down to help Autumn with her shoes.

"We'll be right there," Lois said.

We had all decided to wear the power color, red. Even Baum had on a red tie.

Once we were finally all grouped together and in our organized formation, Baum, Autumn, her family, and the legal team took a slow moving stroll across the street to the courthouse while being squeezed by a throng of shouting and light bulb flashing reporters. It was complete chaos.

Once inside, Shawn and Lois weren't allowed in the courtroom as they were possible witnesses. They were stopped at the door and told they had to stay in the hallway.

I was the only one who could go in with Autumn. I was instructed to sit in the designated family pew in the second row. The first row was reserved for federal deputies and eager law students.

A pale-faced girl was ushered to the seat beside me.

"I'm Autumn's aunt," I told her.

"Boris is my father," she said. "My name is Lana."

I flashed on the character Lara in Dr. Zhivago. Like her, Lana had an angelic face and the purest blonde hair.

"Do you live in New York?" I asked.

"No, I go to college in California," she answered.

She was very soft spoken and pleasant. Her eyes were a clear-water blue.

"This whole thing is really ridiculous," she said. "My father hasn't done anything wrong."

We were both born under the sign of Libra, and we mused that our sun-sign stood for the scales of justice which were hanging on the wall over the judge's bench. Lana and I were the only family members to attend the trail. Yosie didn't have any relatives present.

To the side and behind us was seating for the general public. The benches across from us were reserved for the courtroom artists and members of the press. I leaned over to Benjamin Weiser of *The New York Times* and told him, "Ben, I appreciated your recent article on Autumn."

"I try to be fair," he said.

All the local newspapers were represented. A couple of magazines, including *People*, had sent reps, and the tabloid the *Star* was accounted for. Wendy was there from *Dateline* television.

A gated and fenced off area cut the room in two. The jury stand was on the right-hand side of the room. The floor space in between the gate, jury, and judge's stand was cramped with wooden tables, high-backed chairs, and the multi-person teams of the Prosecution and the Defense.

Autumn and Boris were instructed as to which chairs to sit in. Yosie was led into the courtroom wearing a sedated suit and his Jewish Kippah.

Autumn faced the judge's bench, and she was careful not to look at Yosie.

The jury was brought in and then the judge entered.

Court was started with the bailiff announcing to all those present, "The United States against Autumn Jackson."

Autumn sat unflinching.

"Let me give you some brief preliminary instructions before we proceed to the opening statements." Judge Barbara Jones said to the jury. She would drone out these same instructions every day of the trial. "All right, we will now begin with the government's opening statement. Mr. Engelmayer."

Mr. Engelmayer was the federal prosecutor. He started his speech by telling the jury the case was about a plot to extort money from the entertainer Bill Cosby.

"As you will learn, they (Yosie, Autumn, and Boris) were driven by greed. They wanted to get rich quick," he said.

Another half-hour or more would be spent giving background, as well as a good amount of speculation as to what had happened to bring Autumn to court. "The story is set in a hotel room in California. It was there that the defendants met to plan and carry out their scheme,"

Engelmayer explained. "Well, as you will learn they were working together with other people to produce a children's television show. They worked for a company run by Jose Medina, who also went by the name Yosie Medina. He was the show producer, director and scriptwriter. He had rented the hotel room to serve as the headquarters of the show. The problem was, the show was going nowhere. Long after work had begun on it, it was still amateurish. No episodes had been completed; no episodes had been sold. No sponsors had been lined up. No one had been paid. And the show's attempts to get press attention and publicity had fallen on deaf ears. The evidence will show that in early January of this year, the defendants devised another plan to make millions of dollars. But this time the plan was illegal; it involved extortion; it involved making a threat to Bill Cosby."

Engelmayer pointed out the law when he told the jury, "It does not matter whether you threaten somebody with the truth, with a half-truth, or with a lie. Either way, it's extortion. You will see that while Autumn Jackson was the public face of the extortion scheme, she was not acting alone. She had several confederates. One was Boris Sabas, another was her fiancée, Antonay Williams. He was part of the show and he was also part of the extortion plot. The main one was Yosie Medina. He was a major source of ideas for how to intensify the pressure on Bill Cosby."

At the end of the lengthy speech Engelmayer instructed the jury to listen to the evidence, to listen to Judge Jones instructions, and to use common sense. "If you do these things, the government submits that at the end of the case you will find the defendants, Autumn Jackson, Yosi Median and Boris Sabas guilty of all three counts."

A recess was taken and in the judge's robe room Baum told Judge Jones that juror number three appeared to be sleeping.

Mr. Engelmayer added, "Seven was having the same problem."

When it came time for Baum to give his opening remarks he directed them to the jury. His large bulk moved around the small floor space reserved for such presentations. His hands gestured, and his voice raised and lowered. He was expressive when he said, "The evidence will show that Autumn Jackson had no intention whatsoever of engaging in any illegal or unlawful activity and, I might add, uttered no threat to Mr. Cosby's reputation."

He went on to disclose that Shawn told Autumn from a young age that she was Cosby's child. "He is your father." Baum said, emotionally mimicking Autumn's mother. "As a result of her belief, Autumn felt that she possessed certain legal and moral rights which a daughter has vis-à-vis her father. It is this belief which frames her intent in this case. It was not an intent to extort nor was there any intent to threaten. Autumn Jackson realized that she will never be publicly accepted by Bill Cosby as his daughter, and realized that, despite having received some financial support in the past, she would never receive the non-financial benefits of a relationship with her father.

Continuing on, Baum pointed out, "In 1991, Autumn's mother became involved with drugs. Mr. Cosby learned of it and acted, in Autumn's mind, exactly how an anxious father would act. Mr. Cosby called Autumn's grandmother and told her he wanted Autumn to attend a private high school in Florida. Unlike any statements that Mr. Cosby pays for college educations for various students, he suddenly called Autumn's grandmother and said, 'Shawn is involved with drugs, I want to take Autumn out of that environment, and I want to send Autumn to a private high school in Florida.' In the years to come, we will demonstrate through evidence that Autumn and her mother were given gifts by Mr. Cosby. No one extorted gifts from Mr. Cosby. Autumn, of course, was fully aware of these facts, all of which helped to shape her intent for the actions which are the subject of this case."

Baum talked about the fight with her mother over Tony, and how Autumn and Tony had moved out and into her car. He told the jury how Cosby had sent Autumn $3,000 that was not for educational reasons. When that money ran out she talked to Cosby's lawyer, John (Jack) Schmitt, and that he told Autumn that Cosby was not going to talk to her.

"Autumn then contacted Peter Lund, the CEO and president of CBS, not to utter a threat, but in the hope that he would get her father to call her," Baum told the jury. "She never spoke directly to Mr. Lund, and she received no phone call from Mr. Cosby."

Baum explained, "The government made reference to a so called note which they claim is a threat, an extortion note which on January 16, 1997 Autumn Jackson faxed to Bill Cosby's lawyer, John Schmitt. It became clear to Autumn at that period of time, based on her conversations with Mr. Schmitt, that she was never going to be a part of Bill Cosby's life, that he is not only not helping her anymore, but that he is not even talking to her anymore, and that he is turning his back on her."

Baum shared how that was the impetus behind selling her story to the Globe. "You will learn that before finalizing the contract with the Globe, she tried desperately to speak with her father. Then comes the so called extortion note. The evidence will demonstrate that Autumn Jackson wanted Mr. Schmitt to have her father, Mr. Cosby call her at a number she gave to Jack Schmitt, and then, in what the government describes as a threat, she said, 'If I don't hear from you by today . . . I will have somebody else at CBS contact my father.' She did not say, 'I will destroy his reputation!' She said, 'I will have somebody from CBS contact my father for me.'"

Baum gave three questions for the jury to ponder:

1.   Did Autumn Jackson believe that Bill Cosby was and is her father?

2.   Did she believe that she had lawful rights in dealing with her father?

3.   Did she engage in negotiations with Cosby's lawyer with no intent to extort in settlement of those rights?

"After you answer those three questions in the manner which, I suggest, the evidence will conclusively lead you to a window as to the intent of Autumn Jackson, a lawful intent. And after doing that kind of evaluation, you will ask yourself the final question: 'Who is the real victim here?'"

Yosie's lawyer, Mr. Checkman, and Boris's lawyer, Mr. Cueto would also give opening statements. Their statements were shorter, and not as passion ridden as those delivered by Engelmayer and Baum.

Mr. Liman, another of the government's team of prosecutors, called the first witness.

A one-time ballet dancer, temporary office worker, Donna Pillios was sworn in. She sat erect and poised. She had been working part-time at the office of Peter Lund. At that time he was the president and Chief Executive Officer for CBS.

Pillios was asked dozens of mundane questions including, how she would know if there was a voice mail waiting.

"There was a little button on the phone that would light up when there was a message waiting," she told the court.

The questioning would get even more tedious before she was released from the stand. When she was asked how she would describe the tone of a message that Autumn left, Baum made the first objection.

"Sustained," the judge said.

Court adjourned for a lunch break. The crowded courtroom emptied into the hall where Shawn and Lois were waiting. They had been holding a court of their own at the end of the marble-floored hall.

Shawn looked queenly sitting in an oversized leather and wood chair. She was wearing a regal red dress suit. Smoldering eyes matched the raven black of her hair. She waved her hands through the air in wide gestures, and long iridescent white nails gleamed as she talked to reporters. Her mix of faux and real diamond jewelry glittered brightly, just like her smile. You could see how Cosby would have been smitten with her. She was a vibrant and eye-catching woman.

When she saw us, she brushed by those who had been listening to her and taking notes. Lois followed.

The reporters who had been waiting outside, ushered us back to Baum's office where we would get a rushed bite to eat. The tension was high.

Joslin, a young curly-haired law student had been added to the defense team. She came into the lunchroom and told Shawn in no uncertain terms, "You should be waiting here at the office, not sitting in the hallway of the courthouse."

"My baby is facing prison, and I'm going to be there for her," Shawn informed Joslin.

Autumn never said a word, but ate her lunch; the first meal of her day.

Back in the courtroom, a Ms. Graves was called to the stand.

She worked for Crocker Communications which was an answering service Cosby used to screen and receive calls.

Mr. Engelmayer asked her, "What procedures did Crocker follow in terms of relaying messages to Bill Cosby's residence?"

Ms. Graves answered, "The account procedures were to hold the message until he checked in. If it was an important or an urgent message, something that was timely, then we would call the residence and deliver the message over the phone."

It was eventually brought out that Ms. Graves had been asked to produce copies of any messages taken from Autumn, Shawn, or Yosie to Bill Cosby. The only calls recorded over a year's period were from Autumn.

If Yosie had called Cosby he hadn't used that number. I thought it unlikely that he would have a more direct number to call Bill than Autumn would.

Ms. Graves told the court that there had been eight calls from Autumn, and one time she referred to herself as "Autumn Cosby."

A message had been sent back to Autumn to call Jack Schmitt who had handled the trust funds Cosby had set up for Autumn and Shawn.

Cosby had terminated the answering service on the same day he had left the message for Autumn. It seemed odd that he would do that after using the service for ten years. I wondered if one of Autumn's "urgent" messages had been received by the wrong person, such as Cosby's wife Camille, but there was no way of knowing.

After having been "duly sworn" in, Susan Bloom was put on the witness stand. She was a trustee and estates attorney at a law firm called, Patterson, Belknoap, Webb & Tyler. It was the company that handled Autumn and Shawn's trust accounts. She had never met Autumn personally, but she was assigned the task of doling out her funds.

Mr. Engelmayer said to Susan Bloom, "Let me direct your attention now to Thursday, January 2, 1997. Did you speak with Autumn Jackson that day?"

Bloom: "Yes, I did."

Engelmayer: "Who called who?"

Bloom: "She called me."

Engelmayer: "What happened in the conversation?"

Bloom: "She told me that she only had one more day paid up at the motel. She needed money for hotel fees, and for food and tuition."

Engelmayer: "And, what if anything did you say in response," Engelmayer pressed.

Bloom: "I said that she hadn't shown me that she was enrolled in school, she hadn't sent me anything about courses, and she hadn't shown me that she was going to go out and get a job, and therefore I couldn't send her any money."

In actuality, Autumn said she had told Susan Bloom that she was working for *Weedpatch Productions*, and that although she wasn't being paid she wanted to continue to work there.

"Did you say anything to her about her work at *Weedpatch*?" Engelmayer asked.

Bloom: "Yes, I told her working at *Weedpatch* was just not acceptable to me. I had wanted her to go to school to get a sense of responsibility." The graying-haired woman in the gray suit was all business, her answers were curt, and what she wanted was awfully personal for never having met Autumn.

"Objection, your Honor!" Baum sang out.

Engelmayer: "Please only state what you said to her."

Bloom: "Okay. I said it wasn't acceptable."

94

Engelmayer continued, "Please tell the jury what happened in your final conversation with Autumn Jackson."

Bloom: "Yes, I spoke to Autumn Jackson on the telephone. I told her that, while the course work was acceptable, the job at *Weedpatch Production Company* was not, and that if she wanted me to pay for her support and tuition, she was going to have to give up the job at *Weedpatch Production Company*. She told me that this was the last day that she was paid up at the motel. She needed money for rent and for food, that she couldn't go home because her mother had thrown her out of the house, and that she said she always knew that Mr. Cosby was her father, and that if I wasn't going to send her any money, she was going to get it some other way, and she would sell her story to a newspaper or magazine."

Engelmayer: "What story did you understand her to be referring to?"

Bloom: "I understood the story she was going to sell was that Bill Cosby was her father."

Engelmayer: "How did you respond when she said that if you did not send her money she would go to a newspaper or magazine with her story?"

Bloom: "I told her I couldn't talk to her about anything like that, and I got off the telephone."

Engelmayer: "Did you report what she had said to anyone?"

Bloom: "Yes, I immediately went to my partner, Jack Schmitt, and told him the telephone conversation."

"Ms. Bloom, a few final questions: Did Autumn Jackson in any of your dealings with her ever say to you that she believed she was entitled to college expenses to be paid for by Bill Cosby?"

"I object," Baum said.

"No," Bloom said on the heels of Baum's objection.

"No," said Judge Jones. "I will permit it. Go ahead."

Bloom: "No, she did not."

Engelmayer: "Did she ever tell you that she believed she was entitled to have her living expenses paid by Bill Cosby?"

Baum jumped up from his seat. "Objection!"

"Overruled."

Bloom: "No, she did not."

Engelmayer: "Did Autumn Jackson ever tell you that she believed she was entitled to some form of child-support from Bill Cosby?"

Baum was on his feet again. "Objection!" he yelled.

"Overruled!"

Chapter 14

MULTIPLE WITNESSES

Autumn overtook the jukebox at the *White Horse Tavern*. By the end of the second day of the trial she was feeling restless. The dull boredom of the microscopic questioning was agitating and she needed some relief.

"What'll you have?" a Puerto Rican bartender asked. White teeth shined at the center of his grin. He leaned slightly forward.

"I'll have a brandy and coke. What do you want Autumn?"

"Vodka and orange juice." She always ordered her drink that way. She rarely referred to the concoction as a "screwdriver."

Autumn's music selection played. It was a slow romantic tune. She started to move to the sounds. Though she appeared as nothing more than a teenager, a woman within her was waiting to be discovered. Her long neck stretched as she bobbed her head from side to side to the bar-loud music.

Autumn's eyes closed, tuning out everything around her. It was then that I saw her true depth for the first time. She was hovering at the edge of a metamorphosis.

"Who is that on the jukebox?" I asked.

"Tony Braxton," she said. "I have her tape at the apartment."

Autumn had brought a small recorder that she listened to with earplugs. She let me borrow it a couple of times to listen to a "Jewel" tape I had brought.

"I like the music," I told her. "It's very soulful."

Another bartender who looked remarkably like the character Superman poured us a second drink. The drinks were strong that night and Autumn and I laughed a lot. We made friends with the waitresses and even better friends with the bartenders. They knew who Autumn was, we found out later, but they never said a word about what was happening. They made every effort to give her the space she needed to unwind.

Looking up at the bar's television screen I saw Autumn, with me right behind her, on the *New York One* news station. Everyone partied on pretending not to notice. Autumn left her daytime life to the television, and joined in the nighttime party going on.

Spending 24 hours a day with each other would sometimes get tedious. Being at the pub gave us a chance to visit with other folks while still being in the same room where I could keep a watchful eye.

Our trips to the *White Horse Tavern* for our before bedtime cocktail became a nightly affair. We could be amongst our new-made friends, and Autumn could be herself.

When the trial resumed, Christopher Doherty of the *Globe* tabloid was called to the stand.

Mr. Liman asked a set of questions used to obtain information about the witnesses to establish their credibility. He asked where Doherty worked, where he had worked before, so on, and so forth. He also asked him, "Did there come a time when you received a call from a person who wanted to report a story about the actor Bill Cosby?"

Doherty: "Yes, that's correct."

Liman: "Did you ultimately buy the story?"

Doherty: "No, we didn't."

Liman: "When was the first time you received a call about the story having to do with Bill Cosby?"

Doherty: "January 15th."

Liman: "How do you happen to remember that date?"

Doherty: "It was the day before Ennis Cosby, Bill Cosby's son, was murdered."

Doherty had asked Yosie if he had proof that Autumn was Cosby's daughter. Yosie told him he did, and he faxed a legal letter to prove it.

Liman asked, "Did he give you the name of the woman who claimed to be Bill Cosby's Daughter?"

Doherty: "Yes."

Liman: "What name did he give you?"

Doherty: "Autumn Jackson."

The faxed document was a letter from Susan Bloom addressed to Autumn concerning the trust fund Cosby had established.

Doherty told the jury that he went to the Holiday Inn in Burbank and was met by Tony.

"Would you describe the gentleman who squeezed past the door?" Liman asked.

Doherty: "Yes, he was a tall African-American with a baseball cap, he was skinny, and he was wearing dungaree trousers."

Liman: "How did he identify himself?"

Doherty: "He told me he was Autumn's husband, and he would be making the final decision on whether or not the contract would be signed or the story would be done."

The contract was left with Tony to go over.

Liman: "Directing your attention to the next day, January 16, 1997, would you tell the jury what you were doing that day?"

Doherty: "In the morning I had a personal appointment, which I attended. Obviously, I heard the news and realized Ennis Cosby, Bill Cosby's son, had been murdered that previous night."

Liman: "How did that affect your interest in the story that Mr. Medina and Ms. Jackson had offered you?"

Doherty: "Obviously, the story took on a whole new light. I mean, it was events that had made the story a lot more important than it was the previous day."

❝ᑕᕈᐁᔆ❞

When Autumn and I were back at our apartment after another long day in court I asked her, "What did you think of Doherty's testimony?"

"It was okay," Autumn said. "It's Jack Schmitt's I'm worried about."

"Why is that?" I asked, not wanting to hear any surprises in court.

"He can hurt me," she said.

"How?"

"I'm not sure, but he was the one who called the FBI."

I found it amazing how well Autumn had handled the whole thing so far. She was extremely good at hiding her emotions. Talking about Jack was the first case of jitters she had shown.

The next day, when Jack Schmitt took the stand, he looked to be a smallish man. He had slicked back medium brown hair, a full-cheeked face and thick neck. He wore a rather smug smile that made one corner of his mouth turn up more than the other so that he appeared to have a one-sided grin.

Mr. Engelmayer did the questioning and started at the place where Schmitt had received a fax from Autumn. He had Schmitt read a letter that was accompanied by the contract that Doherty had left with Tony. A portion of the letter dated January 16th, read:

As you should know from the light of your experience as the attorney of my father, the only monies that I get from my father are from you. As you may know from the discussion of my budget problems, I need monies, and I need monies now. . .

You and I have always been able to talk to each other, so it is urgent that you contact me to make certain arrangements, and I need to have my father, Dr. William H. Cosby Jr. to call today. If I don't hear from you by today for discussion about my father and my affairs, then I will have to have someone else at CBS contact my father for me. I want to talk to my father because I need money, and I don't want to do anything to harm my father in any way if at all possible to avoid. Enclosed you will find a copy of a contact that someone is offering monies for my story, which is the only property I have to sell in order to survive.

Love, Autumn

In a second fax to Schmitt, Autumn said: *I am wanting to settle once and finally. I am asking for 40 million dollars to settle it completely.*

Engelmayer asked Schmitt, "Did there come a time when you spoke with Bill Cosby?"

Schmitt: "Yes."

Engelmayer: "What if any instructions did Bill Cosby give you?"

Schmitt: "He told me that I should report what had been happening to the FBI."

Engelmayer: "Did there come a time later that day when you met with agents of the FBI?"

Schmitt: "Yes."

Engelmayer: "At the meeting at the United States attorneys' office what did you tell the agents?"

Schmitt: "I told them that Mr. Cosby was the victim of extortion, I told them that Autumn Jackson was attempting to extort money from Mr. Cosby, told them who she was, and I told them some background about Shawn."

Engelmayer: "After you related that to the FBI what did you do?"

Schmitt: "I went with an FBI agent to a room at the United States Attorney's office that was equipped with some recording devices, and I attempted to call Autumn Jackson."

Schmitt ended up talking to Autumn three times on January 17th, and Englemayer asked him, "Please summarize what happened in your calls to Autumn Jackson."

Schmitt: "I called Autumn, and I told her that in light of what had happened the prior day with Ennis, that we didn't want anything else burdening Mr. Cosby right now, and I asked her how much money it would take to have no further burdens and she told me $40 million. I told her $40 million was a lot of money. We discussed how much money it would take for her not to carry out her threats. Eventually, we came to the number of $24 million."

Engelmayer: "After you did that what happened?"

Schmitt: "I told Autumn that she would have to come to New York to pick up the money, and that I wanted her to sign an agreement so that I could be sure that in fact she had agreed not to carry out her threats against Mr. Cosby."

The court called for a short break. Lois and Shawn were waiting, as usual, in the hall.

When Autumn and I walked out we saw the press huddled in a circle to make sure their hand-copied quotes were as accurate as possible. No recording equipment was allowed in the courthouse.

We barely had enough time to use the bathroom before we were hurried back into the courtroom.

Baum started his cross-examination. He went back over much of what the prosecution had brought up.

Most of the conversations with Autumn had been recorded, and the jury followed along with the written transcripts that had been entered for evidence.

"I am referring to government Exhibit 34 T, call number three. Do you have that in front of you?" Baum asked Schmitt. "You start off, 'This is Jack Schmitt, it is January 17 at 6:05 p.m.'"

"Yes, sir, I have that," Schmitt replied.

Baum: "Down at the bottom of the first page, you stated in that conversation, 'I am sure you have been following what's been happening to Mr. Cosby and his son over the last day here.' Do you recall saying that?"

Schmitt: "Yes, I do."

Baum: "That was the first reference in any phone call with Autumn Jackson to the death of Ennis Cosby, isn't it?"

Schmitt: "Yes, it is."

Baum: "On page two of that conversation, Mr. Schmitt, you ask

Ms. Jackson how much money she wanted, and she replied, 'You tell me what you think is reasonable.' Is that correct?"

Schmitt: "Yes."

Baum: "And despite your response, in which you said, 'Tell me what you need to get this done,' didn't Autumn begin talking about how upset she was over Ennis's death and why she wanted to settle, as she called it? Do you see that in the transcript?"

Schmitt had Baum repeat himself, and then he answered, "Yes."

Baum quoted Autumn talking to Schmitt. He raised his head and looked Schmitt in the eye. "She (Autumn) said, 'I began to realize what hurt me especially with this is that nobody notified me.' Do you see that?" Baum asked Schmitt.

Schmitt: "Yes, I do."

"Autumn said, 'I had to find out about it on the news. This is somebody who has died, who has part of my blood, and no one even bothered, not even my mother even bothered to call me to inform me about it.' Do you see that?" Baum asked.

Schmitt: "Yes, I see that."

"Now, again, you ask her what she wants, and you tell that $40 million is unreasonable. Do you recall that?" Baum waits for an affirmation, but doesn't get it.

Schmitt: "No, what I said is I think $40 million is a lot of money."

Baum comes back, "And, she responds, 'I am sorry. That was my thinking, so I am asking you, what is your thinking?' Do you recall her saying that?"

Schmitt: "Yes, I do."

Baum: "Did she also say that she cared about this man, that he helped bring her into the world, and repeated twice that the last thing she wanted to do was to hurt him (Bill Cosby).

Schmitt: "Yes."

Baum: "Did Ms. Jackson also say that once this is settled, 'you will never have to see my face or speak to me or hear my voice again?"

Schmitt: "Yes."

Baum: "Normally, from what I have seen with other people, they just slide prices back and forth. Did Autumn say this to you?"

Schmitt: "Yes, she did."

Baum: "Isn't that what is usually done in a negotiation, Mr. Schmitt?"

"Slide prices back and forth?" Schmitt answered with a question.

"Have you ever done that?" Baum asked him.

Schmitt: "Bargain over a price?"

Baum: "Yes."

"Yes." Schmitt affirmed.

When court was adjourned Autumn and I went for a quick dinner with Shawn and Lois. We were glad to get away early. It had been another frustrating day. Schmitt had been cautious, clever, and a force to be reckoned with. Autumn was right to be in fear of his testimony.

The next morning Evelyn Taibi was called to the stand to give a motive to the crime. She would tell the jury that Autumn was looking at million dollar houses and that she wanted to be moved into one by Christmas time.

Engelmayer asked Taibi, "And what if anything, did she say about whether she wanted to buy the Greenhaw house."

Taibi: "They (Autumn and Tony) were set on buying that one. She (Autumn) told me that they really loved the house."

Engelmayer: "When was the last time you spoke to Autumn Jackson about the Greenhaw house?

Taibi: "Early part of December. She said that was the house she wanted, and that she would do whatever to buy that home, whatever was required, whatever it took, she was going to buy that house. She was going to buy it; there was no question about it."

Later Autumn told me, "The real estate woman thought we were trying to buy the house without paying the broker's fee, but, that just wasn't so. She was mad at us and that is why she testified against me."

Whether it was true or not, the woman gave a compelling statement. Her testimony would have more bearing on the case than I would have thought possible.

Chapter 15

COSBY TAKES THE STAND

It was a humid 95 degrees in New York City's bowels—the subway. At only 7:30 in the morning, it was promising to be a very hot and humid day. Autumn and I were waiting for the train that would take us to Lower Manhattan. Sweat was dripping down our freshly showered backs, dampening our clothing.

"Where are your shoes for court?" I asked Autumn, not seeing the plastic bag she usually carried with shoes and hose to match her courtroom outfit.

"Oh! No!" Autumn cried, realizing she had forgotten them. With Cosby due in court it was important that she feel confident. Everything had to be right. "We have to go back," she said. "I thought I had them."

We hurried the mile plus back to the apartment, and Autumn scurried up the four stories to find her shoes.

She came back down without them.

"Where are your shoes?" I asked, thinking she had spaced out while she was upstairs and had forgotten them again. I knew she was nervous about Cosby coming to court. Not because of what he would say, but because she was anxious to see her father.

"I couldn't find them," she said. She was bordering on tears.

"Let's think back," I suggested. "When did you last see them?"

"I was sure I had them when we left this morning."

She remembered bringing down the garbage.

"Could they be in the garbage can?" I asked.

Sure enough, that is where they were.

"It's too late to take the subway," I said. "Let's call a cab."

Autumn trudged back up the multi-flight of stairs to make the call.

We were hot and rumbled by the time we reached Baum's office. As everyone nervously awaited our arrival, Shawn and Lois were reading the latest newspaper reports about the case, and Baum was checking to make sure he had all his notes.

As was the drill, once we were all in the lobby of the legal building we lined up in our formation. Baum and Shawn were on each side of Autumn with their arms linked in hers. Lois and I were behind them. The legal team followed us.

It was a complete zoo of reporters outside. We could hardly walk without tripping. I had a firm grip on Lois to make sure she wasn't knocked down, but she ended up saving me from being unbalanced by an obnoxious reporter who was trying to leap over my shoulder to get a picture of the back of Autumn's head. Even though Baum commanded a wide girth he was being crushed in the crowd. "We're walking slowly so that you can get your pictures," he said loudly. "Please let us through!"

Once we reached the courthouse stairs the security officers helped hold back the mob. When we were inside, the large foyer was filled with reporters, agents, and artists hoping for passes to see Cosby on the witness stand. They watched with interest as we headed to the elevators.

I took my seat next to Lana. My heart was still beating hard from the crushing walk over to the courthouse.

The extra loud hum of an air-conditioner matched the chatter going on in the courtroom. When it was turned off it was like a signal for everyone to be quiet. It was silent when the jurors entered, and then the judge.

About three hours into the day, Cosby was sworn in. He looked gaunt, thin in the checks, his hair was graying and bags showed under his eyes. As the prosecutor shuffled papers, Cosby tapped the microphone in front of the witness stand.

A giggle was suppressed around the crowded room.

Was Cosby there to perform a show? No, he was there to tell the truth as he could remember it. This unfortunate situation had started twenty-two years before, and anyone would be hard pressed to remember every detail.

Liman started the direct examination by asking, "Mr. Cosby what do you do for a living?"

Cosby: "I'm an entertainer."

Liman: "For how long have you been an entertainer?"

Cosby: "About 37 years."

Liman: "Can you list the different types of entertainment that you provide?"

Cosby: "Monologue, stand-up comedy, movies, acting. There was a time when I sang, but that stopped!"

Again, the onlookers had to hold back their laughter.

Cosby: "And I have written books, written stories for television."

Liman: "How did you get started in the entertainment business?"

Cosby: "I was in my sophomore year at Temple University, tending bar. To supplement the sixteen dollars a week I made, I would tell jokes to the customers and they would leave a tip under the ashtray. One day this English couple came back from New York and told me they had spoken to a fellow that owned the Gas Light Café coffee house, and they spoke about me, and they wanted me to go up and audition. I went up and auditioned, and I had the job for the summer, which was $60 a week, 6 days a week from 8:00 in the evening until 4:00 in the morning, and my job description was to break up the monotony of the folk singers."

After covering Cosby's career, Liman asked him about his upbringing and family. Then he moved on to what everyone wanted to hear about, Cosby's relationship with Shawn and Autumn. "Sir, did there come a time when you met a woman named Shawn Thompson?"

Cosby: "Yes."

Liman: "When, approximately, did you first meet Shawn Thompson?"

Cosby: "In the early seventies."

Liman: "Where did you meet her?"

Cosby: "At a hotel in Los Angeles."

Liman: "What happened when you met her?"

Cosby: "I asked her to dance, and we did. Then I asked her for her phone number, I wanted to see her."

Liman: "Did you contact her subsequently?"

Cosby: "Yes. Yes, I did."

Liman: "What happened?"

Cosby: "I called her on the phone. I invited her to Las Vegas to spend time with me."

Liman: "Did you have sex with Shawn Thompson?"

Cosby: "Yes."

Liman: "Were you married at the time you had sex with her?"

Cosby: "Yes."

Liman: "Did your wife know at the time that you were having sex with her?"

Cosby: "No."

Liman: "What happened the last time you contacted Shawn Thompson?"

Cosby: "The last time I contacted Shawn Thompson was when I called her. She came to Las Vegas. This was the second time. We were in the living room, on the 30th floor of the Hilton Hotel. We were talking. It was in the daytime. Shawn showed me a picture of a child and she said, 'This is your daughter.'"

Liman: "What did Shawn say the name of the child was?"

Cosby: "Autumn."

During the questioning about Shawn, Cosby directed his answers to the jury. Initially, he avoided looking in Autumn's direction.

Liman led into questions about the money. "Sir, from the mid 1970's forward, after you ended your affair with Shawn Thompson, did you have any contact with her?"

Cosby: "Yes."

Liman: "In general, who initiated the contact?"

Cosby: "Ms. Thompson."

Liman: "Would you describe the contact you had with her?"

Cosby: "Shawn, in the beginning, discussed with me a want or a need to borrow money. Within the borrowing of the money was always the story about Autumn being my child and how she didn't want to hurt Camille's feelings."

Liman: "Would you describe what you mean by that, sir?"

Cosby: "'Bill, I need some money, I need $200, and I don't mean to bother you, but I'll pay it back.' Then would come the part about Autumn being my daughter, and the fact that she hasn't told anyone."

Liman: "How did you respond initially when Shawn Thompson said that Autumn was your daughter?"

Cosby: "I did a lot of just trying to male out-base her by saying that it is not my daughter. We would go back and forth . . . then she would cry, and she would, while crying, say she wanted to borrow the money, she didn't mean any harm, but she needed $200."

Liman: "Did there come a time that you stopped arguing with Shawn Thompson?"

Cosby: "Yes. Because. . .yes."

Cosby's eyes swept across the table to where Autumn sat.

Autumn's eyes hadn't moved from him.

The whole scenario was like the *Wizard of Oz* gone badly. Autumn sat in the courtroom clicking her heels together, but her wizard—believed to be her father, was telling her she had never given him a happy moment. There was not going to be a happy ending.

I looked for similarities in their appearance as if it would prove his paternity. She looked like him in some ways, like Jerold Jackson in others. Only a blood test would provide the truth.

Liman continued, "When Shawn Thompson asked to borrow money and mentioned that Autumn was your daughter, how did you respond?"

Cosby: "The yelling and the crying between the two of us got to the point, and this was always over the telephone, it just got to the point where I no longer wanted to yell over the phone. There was nothing I could win. There was nothing. So Shawn can call and she can ask for money, and I will do whatever I can emotionally. Sometimes I would say, 'well I don't have it,' and then I would call back and then send it to her. There were times when I just felt I didn't want to send it to her anymore and that's it. I remember one time I told my assistant, when I was doing the *Cosby Show*, I said, 'Tell her not to ever call here again.' My assistant came back a half hour later and said, 'Shawn Thompson just called and asked, 'Does that mean forever?' So I just couldn't. There was no cutting it off."

Cosby was throwing invisible daggers in Autumn's direction. It was like he was looking at Autumn, but I wondered if he was thinking of Shawn. I also wondered where he would have been looking if Shawn had been allowed in the room.

Liman: "You just gave it to her?"

Cosby: "Yes."

Liman: "You mentioned that at first she asked to borrow money. Did Shawn Thompson ever pay you back?"

Cosby: "Oh, no. Yes, she never paid me back."

Liman: "After a while did the form of her requests change from borrowing?"

Cosby: "Well, she would say 'I need,' but she stopped talking about paying back. 'I need . . . I need . . . I need!'"

Cosby focus stayed honed in on Autumn, looking her square in the face. I had this image of green bile spewing out of his mouth and gushing all over her.

He knew little about the young woman sitting before him. He had no idea how much, and for how long, she had unconditionally loved and revered him.

Autumn sat unmoving and unflinching before the man she knew to be her father. She wanted his love, and his forgiveness. I didn't see any mercy in his eyes. It looked as if he was shooting out bullets of hate directed right at her heart.

After quizzing Cosby about the forty thousand dollar a year trust fund he had set up for Shawn potentially for life, Liman asked, "Besides giving Shawn Thompson money, did you arrange for Shawn Thompson to go to the *Betty Ford Center* (specialized substance abuse treatment facility)?"

Cosby: "Yes."

Liman: Did you pay for the expenses at the *Betty Ford Center*?"

Cosby: "Yes."

Liman asked, "Did there come a time when you met Shawn Thompson's daughter Autumn Jackson?"

Cosby: "Yes."

Liman: "How many times have you met her?"

Cosby: "Once, I believe."

Liman: How old was she when you first met Autumn Jackson?"

Cosby: "Autumn had to be in high school, I guess 16, 17."

Liman: "What were the circumstances under which you met Autumn Jackson?"

Cosby: "I was at the studio, Kaufman Astoria. Autumn and her grandmother were on their way to Florida from California, and I arranged for them to stop off, visit me, and then head on to the prep school at Florida A&M."

Liman: "When Autumn came to New York, would you describe what happened then?"

Cosby: "When she came to New York, she and her grandmother were brought to my studio. It was on a tape day, which is a Thursday. I have a dinner every Thursday, and invite people to the dinner, of a party of about 12, in my dressing room. . .between shows, 4:30 p.m. and 7:30 p.m. I had a chance to talk to her, and I talked to her about an education. I talked to her about the conditions in her home, but not in a negatory way . . ."

Liman: "How did Autumn respond?"

Cosby: "She was very, very, positive."

Liman: "How long was the visit?"

Cosby: "Maybe from, let's say six hours at the most. Six to eight hours at the most."

Liman: "And did you spend the six to eight hours continuously with her?"

Cosby: "No. No. I took her down the hallway, showed her make-up, showed her hair, showed her wardrobe, and introduced her to the kids. Then I took her on the set to show her that the furniture was actually real and that she could touch things—look at the audience. She had a picture for me of herself, and I took the picture, and I said, 'I'm going to put this picture on my set of the Cosby show, and when the show is going on, you will see this picture of you. This is to inspire you to go on and become somebody. And be something.' She smiled and said, 'Yes.'"

The questioning when on. Liman asked, "During the years of paying for Autumn Jackson's prep school and college educational expenses, did you speak to her?"

Cosby: "Yes."

Liman: "Over the phone or in person?"

Cosby: "Over the phone."

Liman: "How often?"

Cosby: "Maybe fifteen times."

Liman: "What did you say to Autumn Jackson?"

Cosby: "It was 'rah rah sis boom bah. . . Look, you get yourself an education,' and then I would use an example of the situation she was in when she was living with her parent, 'that this is the reason why you're down here, so you don't have to look after your siblings.'"

Cosby continued to look at Autumn. Though his intensity had softened, he was taking advantage of the opportunity to speak his mind about everything that had happened. "And I tried not to make it rough and hard and go . . . drive against her parent. But she, we both connected, I felt, on the phone, over the fact that she knew what I was talking about, that this education would keep her from having to compromise in a way that she was actually living when she was at home . . .And I would say 'call me.' Then one day I said to her, 'Look Autumn, I will tell you this, I am not your father, but I will be, for you, a father figure. You call me; I'm open 24 hours a day. Let me know what you need, what you want.'"

However as Liman continued the questioning it would be brought out that Cosby was not available to her, and he refused as many as eight calls from her until she made a call using his name.

Liman asked, "Did you return the call that you got from the person who identified herself as Autumn Cosby?"

Cosby: "Yes."

Liman: "Can you explain why you returned the call?"

Cosby: "Jackson, Jackson, Autumn, Autumn, and now Cosby. That's not her last name. And I know who Autumn is. And as far as I'm concerned, she is making some sort of threat."

Baum jumped up, "Objection your Honor!"

"Overruled."

In a cross examination by Yosie's attorney, Mr. Checkman asked Cosby, "If I were to give you a number, would you possibly remember that?"

Cosby answered, "Let's try."

Checkman: "Okay."

Cosby: "I'm under oath."

Checkman: "Area code (818) 845-XXXX.

Cosby: "I need four more numbers now."

Checkman: "Extension 3201."

Cosby answered with a resounding, "BINGO!"

Cosby's off color remark synched it. The reporters had the show they had come to watch.

When the examinations were finished, Cosby was whisked out of the courtroom the same way he had been brought in, through a secret elevator used by the federal agents. Shawn had thought he would have entered the courtroom like the rest of us did. She had dressed and combed her hair to perfection.

We broke for lunch. Autumn and I heated water for our usual *Cup of Noodles*. Shawn and Lois sat in the lunch room with us. "I can see some similarities in your looks," I told Autumn. You have the same eyebrows and your fingers are shaped the same.

"She looks just like Bill," Shawn piped in. "They both have tree trunks for thighs."

"Are you disappointed to have not seen Bill," I asked Shawn. Her eyes weren't sparkling with the anticipation they had been earlier.

Shawn was holding her head up high. "Not at all; it was better that way."

We all thought she was fibbing, but we didn't say anything. She and Cosby had a twenty-two year relationship that had gone bust. I assumed she would have loved to have seen him one more time. I would have if I had been in her situation. Unrequited love is a powerful emotion, if that is indeed what she felt. On the other hand, she could have been feeling a good dose of anger toward the entertainer for calling the FBI in on her (their?) daughter. Those feelings may have sparked a scene if she had decided to lay into Cosby. That would have certainly resulted in more fodder for the tabloids.

Before court was called to order, Baum went into the robe room to talk to the judge. He was fighting for a chance to impeach Cosby's testimony and discredit his statement.

Judge Jones wasn't willing to throw out Cosby's testimony, but she did brief the jury when court resumed. "You have heard from Bill Cosby that he told Shawn Thompson and Autumn Jackson that he is not Autumn Jackson's father. This testimony was not offered or admitted to prove the truth of that statement. Whether or not Bill Cosby is Autumn Jackson's father is not an issue that you should consider."

However, that was exactly the issue in Autumn's mind. She had always believed Cosby was her father, and still believed he was. If she just wanted his money she could have kept doing what he wanted her to do, and most likely he would have taken care of her financially for the rest of her life. He had already been supporting her, bought her a car, and was sending money pretty much whenever she wanted.

Instead, she was acting out as a call for Cosby's attention, even if it was in a negative way. For Autumn it was the need to be loved, or let go. She was the revolting child that cried, "Love me or else!"

It was the "or else" that had her tied to a courtroom full of jurors deciding her fate. This was not about money at all. Rather it was about the complicated relationship between parent and child, love and attention.

Chapter 16

ATTRACTING WEIRDO'S

A potential stalker showed up the morning Cosby came to the trial.

While Autumn was making her usual walk across the street, shrouded by the ever present reporters, there was a young man sitting on top of a van. He was dressed unfashionably for New York, wearing shorts, a tee shirt, and hiking boots. A large over-stuffed backpack was sitting next to him. He was singing, *"Sweet dreams, baby . . ."* as we approached.

When we broke for lunch and started our march back across the street to Baum's office, this newcomer came out of nowhere, and jumped in between me and Autumn. I pushed him away from her.

"Get away from Autumn!" I yelled with authority.

He was still waiting outside when we exited the courthouse at 5:00 p.m.

"I was sent here by God!" He shouted out.

The next day, he was in the courtroom sitting right behind me. He looked like he was a mix of white and black nationalities. He had light brown skin and wavy hair. He wore glasses, and I could see gold drenched green eyes behind them.

During a break, the freakish man jumped up and tried to approach Autumn. The bailiff reprimanded him.

"Can't you kick him out of here?" I asked the bailiff.

"No, the trial is open to the public. I can't do anything unless he tries something."

"So he has to stab her first," I said under my breath as I turned on my heel and walked away.

The stalker was present for the rest of the trial. Every time Autumn went to leave the courtroom, I was sure to see that friendly bodies surrounded her, hindering any further attempts of approach.

Most of the press had left the room when Sid Macaraeg was called to the stand. Baum had not managed to get Sid to testify on Autumn's behalf, in fact, it was the prosecution that had won him over. He was the only one working for Yosie who had not been indicted, and he was running scared.

Baum started the cross-examination. "Mr. Macaraeg, I am curious about something. Perhaps you can clear this up. On two occasions yesterday, and on one occasion today, you used the same exact words. You talked about a scheme to extort money. Do you recall that?"

Macaraeg: "Yes."

Baum: "You rehearsed your testimony with the government right?"

Macaraeg: "I don't know if rehearse is the right term for that."

Baum: "Well, they asked you the questions they were going to ask at the trial, right?"

Macaraeg: "Yes."

Baum: "And you went through the answers?"

Macaraeg: "My answers, yes."

Baum: "How many occasions did that take place?"

Macaraeg: "I probably met with Mr. Engelmayer four or five times."

Baum: "How many hours would you say you spent doing those kinds of things?"

Macaraeg: "Sometimes two, sometimes four hours."

Baum: "In each session, right?"

Macaraeg: "Yes."

Baum: "And did they caution you, request you, or otherwise direct you to use the term 'a scheme to extort money?"

Macaraeg: "They did not direct me to do that, no."

Baum: "But you discussed those, that term specifically, didn't you?"

Macaraeg: "Yes, because it is stated in my agreement with the United States government."

Baum: "So you wanted to say the same words that were in the agreement?"

Macaraeg: "I used the same words."

Baum: "So in other words, the words that you wanted to convey to the jury were the words that were in the agreement drawn up by the U.S. Attorney's Office, right?"

Macaraeg: "I thought it was appropriate, yes."

Baum: "Mr. Checkman asked you about the occasions that you were present when no one discussed any extortion or blackmail. Do you recall that question?"

Macaraeg: "Yes. Those words were not used."

"Ah, those words were not used," Baum echoed.

Since Shawn couldn't enter the courtroom, she continued to entertain the reporters who missed getting into the courtroom before the doors closed for the session.

When the judge dismissed everyone for the day, Baum took the legal team, Autumn, Lois, Shawn, and me all out to dinner.

On the way home, Autumn and I took a couple of deep breaths of fresh air before heading down into the dungeon like subway. Once we were underground there was a woman playing a violin for spare change. The classical tune reminded me of a number I had danced to in a ballet recital as a child.

The hallways were empty, so I struck up a ballet pose and started pirouetting across the floor.

Autumn caught me at it, and started to laugh.

"You're too much," she said, and she continued laughing.

With all the heaviness that Autumn had to go through, it was good to see her laugh at my shenanigans. She needed to have something to laugh about.

Later on, she would buy me a silver ring in the shape of a ballerina.

The next day Baum continued his questioning of Sid Macaraeg. "When you found out about the arrest of Autumn and Mr. Medina, you were very surprised weren't you?"

Macaraeg: "Yes, I was."

Baum: "Because you didn't do anything wrong, you didn't commit a crime, did you?"

Macaraeg: "Not that I knew of, no."

Baum: "When you signed the agreement, the point of the agreement was that you wouldn't be charged for anything having to do with the case."

Macaraeg: "Yes. With the assistance that I had provided to them, yes."

Baum: "And it was a condition, was it not, that you testify in this trial?"

Macaraeg: "It was one of the things that I was supposed to do, yes."

After asking other similar questions, Baum directed his inquisition to the issue of Yosie Medina. "It was tough to say 'no' to Mr. Medina, wasn't it?"

Macaraeg: "Yes."

Baum: "He was very dominating."

Macaraeg: "Yes."

Baum: "He wanted everything done his way."

Macaraeg: "Yes."

Baum: "He was very controlling."

Macaraeg: "Yes."

Baum: "And you considered him to be very knowledgeable, didn't you Mr. Macaraeg?"

Macaraeg: "I did consider that, yes."

Baum: "You trusted him."

Macaraeg: "Yes."

Baum: "The same as Autumn trusted him, right?"

Macaraeg: "Yes."

A letter was submitted to evidence, and again Baum continued his questions. "At one point in your testimony you said that you heard Autumn say something about a settlement, and the words 40 million. Do you recall that?"

Macaraeg: "Yes."

Baum: "And isn't it a fact that, at that point, Yosie was sitting next to her, instructing her?"

Macaraeg: "Yes."

Baum: "And, if fact, he was writing on a piece of paper for her?"

Macaraeg: "Yes."

Baum: "And did you observe that she was following those instructions?"

Macaraeg: "Yes."

In conclusion, Baum asked, "Until Autumn called you after the arrest, isn't it true that extortion never came to your mind?"

Macaraeg: "Yes."

§⊃⌒◌₅

We were given a day off from court that everyone needed. Shawn, Lois, Autumn and I planned a shopping trip. When we went to pick up Lois and Shawn at their hotel, Shawn started talking about when Cosby would call her.

"One night Bill called me up and told me he wanted me to wear my hair like a movie star's he had seen on the television."

"He told you how to wear your hair?" I asked.

"He told me what to do all the time. He would call me at two or three in the morning and tell me, 'I want you to do this . . . I want you to do that.'"

When we arrived at the street where we wanted to start shopping,

Autumn was well known by passersby. How could she not be? She was on the front page of every paper every day, and in several of the major magazines. You could turn on the television day or night and see her strutting across the screen every hour on the hour.

While we were shopping, the streets were extremely crowded. Shawn, Autumn, and Lois walked ahead while I walked behind.

We passed by a loud-mouthed African-American man who spotted Autumn.

"Hey! Autumn! Hey! Stop! I want to talk to you!" He was coming up behind us waving an unlit cigarette.

"Hey, Autumn, I know who you are!"

Autumn was in front of me and when he tried to get past me, I pushed my body against his and held out my elbow against his chest to stop his 250-pound bulked up body from passing.

"Let me by," he said. "I want her autograph."

"She isn't giving any autographs," I said forcefully, as if we were the same size.

Though he could have pushed by me easily enough, he seemed to find my elbow an adequate barrier.

Then he started yelling obscenities. "Autumn, you're a cocaine-whore drug-using bitch!"

"Autumn, start walking faster!" I yelled. I didn't know how much longer I was going to be able to hold off the brute.

Fortunately, a policeman happened by, and saw what was happening.

The offensive man dropped back.

Autumn turned around and gave me a big smile. "Good job, Aunt Jewel!"

ⓢⓒⓙⓞⓢ

After we had returned home and were getting ready for bed I went in to brush my teeth. When I came out of the bathroom Autumn told me, "My mom just called and said she's on her way over to spend the night. She and grandma just had a fight."

"Oh no she's not," I said, and I called Shawn back. "You're not coming over here and upsetting Autumn."

"Who the hell are you to tell me what I can do?" Shawn yelled and then hung up.

"I can't believe that my mother would fight with grandma," Autumn said. Tears were pooling in her slightly slanted black eyes. She was visibly upset.

Suddenly, we could hear yelling in the street. "Autumn! Autumn!" Shawn was screaming.

The security door was locked at the ground floor so she wouldn't be able to come in.

"Don't open that door," I warned Autumn. I didn't want to argue with Shawn or have Autumn upset any more than she already was. She sure didn't need another case of hives.

"Don't worry I won't."

In a couple minutes the phone was ringing. Shawn had gone to a phone booth.

"Get a room for the night and cool off," I told Shawn. It had been more than a few grueling days of court and emotions were high for everyone, including Shawn. She may not have been on the indictment, but her name was coming up plenty in the trial.

She asked to talk to Autumn, so I handed her the phone.

"Come out and talk to me." Shawn implored her daughter.

"No, I can't," said Autumn.

"You mean you're telling me, 'No!'"

"That's right," Autumn replied. "I'm telling you: No!"

It was probably the first time Autumn had ever exerted herself against her mother so forcefully.

Shawn hung up on her.

It was a growing moment for Autumn, and a devastating one for Shawn.

Autumn called her grandmother, called to check their hotel security, and even called Shawn's current husband, Darrell Upshaw, to ask him to get Shawn under control.

When Shawn walked into Baum's office the next day, she tried to win Autumn's sympathy by telling her, "I thought about jumping off a bridge." In the next breath, she calmly said, "I'm going to kill Jewel."

Shawn saw me as the barrier to keeping control of Autumn, and although she was partially right, I was incensed that she would threaten my life. I was helping her daughter through a terrible ordeal.

"She threatens to kill everyone that gets in her way," Autumn told me. "She thinks everyone is trying to take me away from her, but she's the one pushing me out of her life."

When Cosby had brought Autumn and Lois to New York for their visit, Lois had made a video tape that was used as evidence. It showed Cosby with his arm around Autumn while they were talking.

Lois never consulted Autumn if she would like to have the taped video once it became worth a lot of money. Autumn's debts were certainly growing, and she could have used a windfall. Instead, after Lois and Shawn had made up, she gave Shawn the video to sell.

"Your mother sold your video," I told Autumn.

"Yeah, and she wasn't even in it," Autumn said.

❧

Lois was called to the stand in Autumn's defense.

Baum asked Lois, "Do you know Shawn Thompson Upshaw?"

Lois answered, "That's my daughter."

Baum: "In the fall of 1973 into early 1974, where were you living?"

Lois: "In Los Angeles."

Baum: "And who was living with you?"

Lois: "Shawn."

Baum: "During this period of time, was Shawn pregnant?"

Lois: "Yes, she was."

Baum: "During this period of time, did you ever speak with Cosby?"

Lois: "Yes, he called the house many times."

Baum: "And, during this period of time, when Shawn was pregnant, do you know if she ever went to meet with Mr. Cosby?"

Lois: "Yes. In fact, she used my car."

Baum asked Lois, "Did you ever talk to Autumn about what Shawn had told you following that meeting with Mr. Cosby?"

Lois: "Yes."

Baum: "And how old was Autumn at the time, do you recall?"

Lois: "She was five or six, and getting ready for school."

Baum: "And what did you talk to Autumn about?"

Lois: "One thing was about her birth certificate, and the other was about who her father was."

Baum: "And what did you tell her?"

Lois: "That her father was Bill Cosby."

Baum: "And, what did you tell her about her birth certificate?"

Lois: "That she, her mother (Shawn), was told not to put his (Cosby's) name on the birth certificate. And, so that's why Jerold Jackson's name was on the birth certificate."

118

Baum: "And sometime after that, when Autumn was growing up, did you also tell Autumn what Mr. Cosby had said, if Shawn put Jackson's name on the birth certificate?"

Lois: "Yes, I did."

Baum: "What did you tell Autumn?"

Lois: "That as long as she didn't tell anyone about it, that he (Cosby) would take care of her mother and her, and take care of his responsibility."

Chapter 17

THE VERDICT

As to Count 1, we the jury find the defendant Autumn Jackson, GUILTY!

As to Count 2, we the jury find the defendant Autumn Jackson, GUILTY!

As to Count 3, we the jury find the defendant Autumn Jackson, GUILTY!

The clerk continued on, reading the guilty verdicts for Jose Medina and Boris Sabos, but the real interest had been in Autumn's judgment.

Autumn had hoped beyond hope that the jury would realize the good in her. Even though there was a mountain of evidence against her she had prayed they would see the sincerity in her heart, how others had conned her into the actions she had taken, and how she would never hurt Bill Cosby intentionally.

It's a funny thing about the connection between parent and child. Unconditional love, is just that—unconditional. No matter what wrong is committed toward a child they love their parent anyway. Even though Shawn had terrified Autumn by leaving the house and not guaranteeing a return, Autumn would always love her for no other fact than Shawn was her mother.

Though Autumn barely knew Cosby, she believed he was her father, and she loved him unconditionally. I could tell by the way she would talk about him—a reverence in her voice, a hopeful glint in her eye. There was no way she wanted to hurt him, even though she suffered complete disappointment in his lack of caring. If only he would have talked to her with a sincere interest, perhaps they could have worked things out. Forget the "rah rah sis boom bah. . ." stuff. If he had taken the time to find out what was in the child's heart, or in this case, the young woman's heart, there could have been a whole different ending.

❧

The day the defense rested, everyone on the team showed up tired or not feeling well.

After the council met with the judge, Baum said, "Most judges side with the prosecution. Judge Jones tied my hands at every turn."

Ed from Autumn's defense team was fuming and furious. "I told the judge that what she expected was unprecedented."

Judge Jones was going to bypass the legal explanation of extortion and simply tell the jury it would be extortion if Cosby felt threatened, which he already said he had.

"The judge is just trying to keep her job," Autumn sympathized.

"I'm glad you are able to keep such a good attitude," I said, surprised at Autumn's generosity. If it had been my life on the line I would have been extremely upset.

The judge gave her instructions to the jury and they went into their deliberating room to decide Autumn's fate. The rest of the court broke up into small groups.

The prosecutor Mr. Engelmayer was so self-assured and relaxed he had his feet up on one of the tables.

Autumn, Shawn, Lois and I sat at the family bench, and conversed about anything and everything that entered our minds, except why we were there. One of the court artists drew a picture of Autumn, Shawn, and me talking.

I could see discouragement setting into Autumn's face as the jury requested different bits and pieces of the evidence against her.

The next day the waiting continued. Baum came in hopeful of a mistrial. "There was an anonymous phone call," he told us. "Juror number 3 was at a Yankee's game and was asking the surrounding fans how they would judge the case." The juror in question had appeared to be sleeping through most of the closing statements. It was no wonder he was asking for help.

However when the judge questioned him, he said he hadn't asked anyone's opinion and she let it slide. If he had been honest, the whole thing would have been thrown out of court. Autumn could have gone home, and put the nightmare behind her.

As the hours rolled by, Autumn took to playing a game. She selected an animal that reminded her of each of us. I joined in helping her make the selections. She thought Robert was like a penguin, Checkman a giraffe, and Liman a fish. We decided she was a Kuala bear, Shawn was a jaguar, and I was a peacock. And so the game went.

When she tired of that we played a game of what actor would play who for a "made for TV" movie. There had been offers enough to do one, but Richard put his foot down on that happening. He didn't want the sordid details out any more than they were already.

"Halle Berry could play you," I told Autumn.

"And Will Smith could play Tony," Autumn countered.

"How about Cher for me?"

"No, Jill Clayburgh would be better, you're kind of funny like she is."

"Richard wants to be played by Clint Eastwood, but I think Tom Skerritt would be better," I said.

"What about my mother? Who do you think should play her?" Autumn asked.

"I don't know . . . someone loud," I suggested.

We laughed.

The game was interrupted when we were told we could go home for the day.

That night it was raining, and it was hard not to feel that the rain was a bad sign. Autumn and I went to the *White Horse Tavern*. She was emotionally exhausted. She was sitting on a seat at the corner of the bar drinking a glass of water. Since there was nothing to celebrate she had forgone her nightly cocktail.

As was my protective way, I was just about to tell her to trade seats with me, putting her to the inside, when a woman in a trench coat appeared in the crowd, and produced a camera.

Flash! Flash!

It was like lightening going off. Autumn sat stunned and I held out my hand in front of the woman's camera lens. "Stop!" I shouted.

"Who are you?" the photographer demanded to know.

"I'm her aunt."

Flash! The camera went off again.

I started yelling for the bartender who was on his way over the bar to throw her out.

"I'm so sorry," he said, apologizing to Autumn. "I didn't see her come in."

The damage was done. The next day one of her candid pictures showed up in the paper announcing that Autumn liked to hang out at the *White Horse Tavern*. Her little bit of privacy was diminishing.

After three days of deliberations the jury marched back into the courtroom. When the guilty verdict was read Autumn began to cry hysterically. Great sobs racked her shoulders, and the only words she was able to utter were to Baum, "How could they do that? How could they?"

I was brought forward to help Autumn fill out the necessary forms assuring her continued release until the sentencing date, as well as the continuation of her bail-bond. Richard and I wouldn't be receiving back the titles to our property just yet.

Autumn was sobbing so hard, the most she could do was hold up her slender fingers to answer my questions about addresses and phone numbers. Since that information had been posted in the newspaper, I would have thought they already knew it, but you do what they tell you to do when the court asks it, so I filled out the necessary paperwork without question.

Autumn cried on as the courtroom emptied. Lois, Shawn, and I watched as the young woman turned inside out. Her mouth was wide open and her soul floated right out. Just as Bill had unleashed a lifetime of frustration in her direction, she let loose a flood that no dam could hold back. An hour went by before Autumn's sobs started to subside. She could barely lift herself up to walk out. Shawn and Lois supported her shaky steps. Federal agents led us to the special elevator Cosby had used. It would take us to an underground tunnel leading to the next building. It was there that Autumn would fill out more papers and check in with a parole officer.

When we arrived at the holding room, Baum was there waiting to tell Autumn how sorry he was at losing the case. "I knew it was going to tough," he said. He seemed disoriented himself. He reviewed the trial trying to figure out what he could have done differently, and how he could make everything okay when it was as bad as it could be.

Lana was there waiting for her father, who had also been found guilty. We would find out later, that it wasn't the jury's decision about Autumn that had taken 3 days, but Boris' involvement which was driving Yosie and Autumn to the airport.

Lana was crying. "This is so unfair," she whimpered. "All he did was give them a ride."

Autumn, who had only moments earlier been lost to her own despair, went to Lana and started stroking her hair. "It's okay," Autumn said pushing her own emotions aside. "Everything's going to be okay."

When we were with the parole officer she told Autumn that she wouldn't be allowed to contact Cosby for any reason—under any circumstances.

Even though Autumn hadn't been sentenced yet, they already had a list of things she couldn't do. The list was read to her, and then she had to sign a copy of their paperwork.

We left the building with special agents surrounding us. Camera's clicked away as we were ushered into a car that would take us home.

Autumn reached over and squeezed my hand, again reaching past her own sense of pain.

When we arrived at our apartment I asked, "Was there any time during all of this that you wondered if you had done something wrong?"

"No, never," she said, still believing her innocence.

What she had done wrong was to have trust in those who were not looking out for her best interest, but rather their own.

We had a couple of days before we would be heading back home. We went out shopping and stopped at *Caliente's* for lunch.

I saw a woman who was overly curious about Autumn. When we left the restaurant Autumn spotted a camera focused on us from across the street. We assumed the woman has called the press.

We had some shopping to do. One of the stops was at a smoke shop so Autumn could get a pack of her little cigars.

The man with the camera followed us for several blocks. I didn't want him following us back to our apartment, so I told Autumn we needed to jump into a cab. While we were trying to flag a cab a girl walked up to us who we had met earlier at the *White Horse Tavern*. By the time a cab stopped, the camera man had caught up with us and he was snapping pictures. We jumped in the cab and had the driver circle around until we were sure we had lost him. The driver let us off a block from our place.

Later it would come out in the *Globe* tabloid that we had gone into a cigar shop so that Autumn could buy rolling papers for marijuana, and that I was taking her gay-bar hopping. Nothing could have been farther from the truth.

The night before we left New York, Autumn and I sat down on the front stoop together. It was late and still very warm out.

We talked about all the things that women like to talk about: men, sex, marriage, and babies.

"The first real friend I ever had was named Jewel," Autumn said.

"And now we're friends," I offered.

We had spent the past thirty days together without a single argument. The worst it had come to between us was if we would rather eat Chinese, her favorite, or Italian which was mine. We had functioned well together despite all the scary, bizarre, painful, and crazy stuff going on.

When we arrived at the airport to go home, Autumn's face was on every television in the waiting areas. A policeman asked us if we wanted to wait for our flight in a private lounge and we accepted.

When we laid over in Phoenix, again Autumn was the top news item covering the screen of the waiting area televisions.

Just before landing at the Sacramento airport Autumn fixed her makeup and combed her hair in preparation to greet Tony.

During the two-hour ride back to Autumn's grandmother's house she filled Tony in about the overwhelming press, her overwhelming mother, and the overwhelming verdict.

The next day, I called over to Lois's house and Autumn was still sleeping. Lois answered the phone and I asked her, "Has Autumn said anything to you about getting married?"

"No, but I know she wants to have a big wedding."

That night Autumn and Tony came to dinner.

"What's happening with your case?" I asked Tony.

"My lawyer is supposed to be calling me."

Autumn told Richard, "Tony and I are going to tell you what we're going to do about getting married."

They wanted to get married in Florida where Tony's family was.

Richard and I weren't totally convinced that they wouldn't run, especially now that Autumn had been found guilty. I never had the sense that Autumn would disappear, but between her and Tony I wasn't sure what they might decide.

Richard called Baum and told him, "I don't want to have to go running through the sugar-cane fields after Tony with a machete."

Baum laughed.

We went to Autumn's grandmother's house to hear their wedding plans. "We want to get married on an island near Florida," Autumn said.

Tony suggested that they film the wedding and sell it to the media.

I produced a copy of the bond we had for Autumn's bail. It said right on it that she wasn't to leave the area. If she did we could have to come up with the quarter of a million dollars that was signed for her release from jail.

"Is this all my life is worth?" Autumn cried. "A quarter of a million dollars?"

"That's what all our lives are worth put together, Autumn," I said, thinking about all the deeds and titles we had to send to the government—promising them everything we owned if she skipped bail.

"I can count all the mistakes I have made in my life on one hand," Autumn said holding up a child-sized hand—her fingers spread apart. "Well, this one mistake was pretty big," she confessed, smiling coyly.

We all started to laugh.

With the ice broken, we were able to talk about what was really feasible, which was her getting married right where we lived in Lake County, California.

Tony was quick to realize that if he wanted to get married he would have to forget about going to Florida.

Autumn was ready to tell the media about her side of the story, and a meeting with *NBC* was set up. She called and asked if I would like to come along to meet with *Dateline* in New York.

NBC had a car waiting at the airport, and we were taken downtown to New York City's Hilton Hotel. It was very nice, and there were even televisions in all the elevators. That fact wasn't to Autumn's advantage though. On more than one ride in a loaded car there would be a close up of Autumn on the screen. During these moments, Autumn wouldn't look down, but rather held her head high and looked straight ahead.

Baum arranged for Autumn to have a psychiatric evaluation while we were there, in hopes that it would help to lessen her sentence.

The interview took three hours, and I used the time to write another bedtime story.

As soon as she was finished we rushed to a restaurant where Wendy had arranged for us to meet with Ed Gordon to discuss the *Dateline* interview. Baum also met us there.

Ed asked Autumn, "What have you learned from this experience?"

Her quick reply was, "I'll be sure to hire a lawyer in the future."

Two of Autumn's condemning jurors told the press that if she had consulted with a lawyer before asking Cosby for money she wouldn't have broken the law.

"That's not the answer I'm looking for," said Ed with paramount seriousness.

Baum told us later that *Dateline* wanted to tape Autumn before sentencing in case she was whisked off to prison. That way they could still air the tape.

"This would be good publicity for any future movie or book," Baum told Autumn.

This whole mess had started over Autumn trying to coax money from Cosby, and the thought of her still trying to find a way to make money on Cosby's fame was beyond me. However, she was accumulating a large amount of debt with all the trips to New York, and she saw a book or a movie as a quick remedy. I hadn't written my book yet.

Before we left New York, Autumn told Baum about her plans to sell her wedding video.

Baum didn't want any unnecessary press that might sway the judge against her before her sentencing. "You'll want to have a clause in the contract that says they won't air it too early, and that still might not be a deterrent from them doing so."

ᔆᑕ᠑᠊ᑐᓵ

After we returned home to Clearlake, Shawn arranged for *ABC* to pitch Autumn as well.

Wanda Akin, whom Shawn had tried to connect Autumn with before, had come to Lake County with Shawn to attend the pitch.

We met with Lisa, the current representative for *20/20*. "I think a family piece would be good," she suggested.

Autumn didn't want to do an interview with Shawn which was the suggestion. Also, Autumn felt intimidated by the idea of being interviewed by Barbara Walters.

"*NBC* will do something negative," Wanda threw in, trying to help Lisa's sale.

"Why do you think that?" I asked.

"Katie Couric wouldn't even do the interview," Wanda said.

"Why do you want to give an interview?" Lisa asked Autumn.

"I want to set the record straight."

The next morning Lisa called me from *ABC*. "It sounds like Shawn loves Autumn," she said.

"That's one thing about Shawn; she loves her children very much," I responded.

"Does Autumn love her?"

"Oh yes, but she's attempting to grow up and cut her strings. She wants to be seen as the adult she is."

Chapter 18

GOLDEN LEAVES

On this day, we are gathered here with friends and family to witness the commitment of two best friends, Tony Williams and Autumn Jackson, by uniting together in matrimony, and to truly become one. . .

The trees were wearing their fall finery, and were covered in gold leaves, a perfect setting for the background of Autumn's wedding day, October 18, 1997.

Autumn's Uncle Ricky and her grandmother had done everything they could to give Autumn what she had wanted her Florida wedding to be, albeit on a lesser scale.

There were several islands in the lake outside her grandmother's house, and Richard had arranged for the wedding to take place on one of them. To mimic the cruise Autumn wanted, a riverboat was rented to do a three-hour tour of the lake. A tropical feast was served on board along with a designer wedding cake with gold flowers.

Around thirty people attended the event, all having to be transported by boat to the island for the ceremony.

Autumn didn't invite her mother or even tell her about the wedding until it was over. She did have her brother, Aaron come up for a visit so that at least he was able to be there. He walked her up a grassy aisle to a white arbor set up for the wedding.

Tony and Autumn exchanged their simple vows of love and friendship that they had written.

Lois had helped Autumn dress for the occasion. I watched as she lovingly fixed her granddaughter's hair into a very becoming style.

Autumn had found the perfect Cinderella shoes that tied in bows around her ankles with satin ribbons. Lois had given her a multi-strand of pearls to wear around her neck that had matching earrings. When Autumn was finished being buttoned into a traditional ivory-colored wedding gown that was decorated with beads and lace, she looked like an Indian princess—Pocahontas perhaps?

After the ceremony, Autumn and Tony signed their wedding certificate. Autumn wrote the word "unknown" in the space asking for her father's name, which was what Baum had suggested.

On the riverboat, a stereo played rap tunes. The all-white guests gyrated to the black music. Autumn's eyes sparkled with love for Tony as they danced the afternoon away.

There was an after party back at the island, and some of the younger guests danced on, or sat by a fire that was burning outside to fend off the cool night air.

The last boat left for the mainland at midnight, leaving Autumn and Tony alone on the island for their wedding night. They stayed in a Japanese styled house fit for newlyweds.

One of the guests had told Autumn, "I always feel so good when I'm around you."

Autumn did have an attractive magnetism. You couldn't help but feel good just being around her. Under different circumstances I think we would have been lifelong friends.

As irony would have it, Cosby was scheduled to do a comedy show at *Konocti Harbor*, a concert resort 5 minutes from where Autumn lived—now as a married woman.

Supposedly, the booking had been made at the resort before any of this had ever happened.

At one time, Lois had worked at the resort, and some of her old co-workers told her Cosby had the grounds searched for Autumn before he would perform.

When we heard he was coming, we talked about going, but none of us had the stomach for it. We had enough of Cosby in our lives. Besides, I don't think any of us would have found anything he said to be funny considering the circumstances.

"I would like to go, just to see my father," Autumn said, "but I know it would cause too much trouble."

Again, Autumn was coming from a place of unconditional love. At the trial the man whom she regarded as her father never gave her a smile, but the chance to just be near him was a huge pull on her heartstrings.

We suspected the press would be there, hoping for just such an occurrence.

Just days before we were to leave for New York for Autumn's sentencing, a *Dateline* crew flew out to start taping her interview.

For the segment Autumn would be doing, they were attempting to show her in her environment. However, it was agreed they couldn't ask her any questions until after she went to sentencing.

We went to a park where Ed Gordon and Autumn walked over a wooden bridge, and then Autumn walked onto a dock where she sat down to feed some ducks.

The trees were starting to lose their golden leaves that had turned color in time for Autumn's wedding. The wind swept the leaves up into swirls around their feet as if on cue for the filming. It was very cold out, and it wasn't long before we were all shivering.

I thought it humorous when they had Autumn sitting on a park bench reading a book for a close up shot. Autumn made it a point to never read anything, at least while we were hanging out together.

When the filming was finished, we went to lunch at the *Konocti Harbor Resort* where Cosby had just performed.

In order to show us what kind of interviews Ed did, Wendy had sent us a copy of an interview he had done with OJ Simpson.

Tony asked Ed if he thought OJ had killed Nicole and Goldman.

"I was wondering when I would get asked that," Ed said. His answer was given, but he said it was "off the record."

"How is Bryant Gumbo's new show going?" I asked.

"It's coming along." Ed answered. "Did you know that they preempted one the of *Public Eye* episodes to show Cosby's appearance in *Touched by an Angel*, for a second time?"

❧⊂❧⤳ᗪ₅

Autumn and I flew back to New York on Dec 4th. We had a very nice 18th floor apartment we had rented for the coming week. It had a large window that lent itself to a great view of the city's skyscrapers. Some of the buildings were decorated with multi-colored lights for the approaching Christmas holiday. Our view of the Chrysler building was magnificent.

When we were sitting back relaxing and recovering from our flight, Autumn told me, "I don't want to do the paternity test."

"It would give you closure," I told her.

"I don't care," she said. "I don't think Mr. Cosby will do the test after sentencing, and Robert doesn't want me to do it before."

She had a faraway look in her eyes and said, "I don't think I'll ever get to know who my father is."

"Do you want to go out?" I asked her. She had never wanted to stay in on any of our other trips to New York, and I wanted to be obliging.

"No," she answered. "My period is due and my breasts hurt."

"Could you be pregnant?" I asked, knowing too well what tender breasts can mean.

"No, but I'm tired. I think I'll go to bed."

Autumn didn't get up until 3:00 the next afternoon. I knew she liked to sleep late, so I didn't think too much about it. We had a day's grace before all the work would begin to get Autumn ready for her sentencing.

The next day Baum told us that Autumn's sentencing has been postponed for a couple of days taking us past the time our rental expired.

I hadn't been prepared for that. Renting an apartment in New York City by the week was not an easy thing to do. I called to see if we could extend our stay but they had other renter's coming in. It was the perfect setup for a bout of *PMS (Pre Menstrual Syndrome)*. On top of everything else; we women had to deal with our hormonal fluctuations.

Autumn and I used the delay to check out New York City's Christmas decorations. We went to see the famous Christmas tree at the Rockefeller Center. Cosby had been the master of ceremonies at the lighting, so we had avoided that as well, not taking any chances that Autumn would be seen in the crowd.

When we were tired of sightseeing, we had something to eat, did a little shopping at the neighborhood grocery, and bought some inexpensive romance videos to watch at the apartment on the VCR.

"I started my period," Autumn told me.

We settled in for a night of movies. It was frosty cold outside, and it was fun to snuggle in.

A second uneventful day passed by. We went to check in at the *White Horse Tavern*. Only a few of our old friends were there. A lot of the others were laid off for the winter season.

It was cold outside and dreary. I was surprised but grateful when Autumn was content to spend another night in our apartment. It was a lovely one bedroom place, much nicer than the one we had stayed in during the trial, and there weren't any snoopy landladies around. I read her another bedtime story I had written.

Autumn didn't like that one very much. It didn't have a happy ending like all the rest. Somehow though, it fit my *PMS* mood. I had to agree *FREE AS A BIRD* was rather dark and depressing. It was perhaps a little too true to life.

The next day Autumn was called in to see Baum. Somehow we missed our subway stop and ended up at a major hub. Everyone in the station was African American.

"Now I'm the minority," I told Autumn. I was the only white person out of hundreds of people waiting for their connections.

"Don't worry," she said. "I know the talk."

Autumn did go back and forth between the black and white worlds since she belonged to both. With me she was a white girl, with Tony she was a black woman speaking in ebonics with all its inflections.

When we arrived at Baum's office he was hung up in court, and the day was basically wasted.

We spent another night watching videos we had picked up for a couple of dollars each.

Finally, by the next day we meet with Baum. He went over what Autumn needed to say at sentencing.

"I have some unexpected news," Baum said. "I received a call from the *National Enquirer* asking if I could back up a story they were called about. Evidently, Jerold Jackson and his wife are splitting up. She came forward to tell the story that Cosby's lawyer was paying off Jackson to say he was Autumn's dad."

Autumn wasn't surprised at all. She and Shawn had been saying that Cosby would stoop to such measures all along. I hadn't wanted to believe it even though throughout the years of being in the family I had heard some rather negative stories.

The caption to the story of Cosby's payoff was called "Rent-a-Pop!" In the article, Jackson confessed to taking ten thousand dollars from Cosby after Autumn's arrest.

In another article it said that Jerold Jackson even received a new car from Cosby.

Eventually, Attorney Jack Schmitt would admit on national television that Cosby gave Jerold Jackson money to pay bills.

Baum was hoping this news would give Autumn a postponement, but the judge didn't think the information was relevant to the case.

"We have to see the Santa at Macy's," I told Autumn.

"I have something to ask him for," she said. "My acquittal!"

When the time ran out that we could stay at our apartment, *NBC* was gracious enough to put us up for a couple of days. Autumn needed to finish up at court after her sentencing, and follow through with the anticipated interview she had committed to give *Dateline*.

When sentencing day arrived, Wendy picked us up in a Lincoln Town Car. We drove by the courthouse steps, and there were flash bulbs going off amid a mass of cameramen moving like a centipede. Baum and Shawn had walked across to court alone, just as Autumn had requested.

We outsmarted the press by going to the side entrance where not even one reporter had thought to be.

We met Baum and Shawn inside.

Shawn gave Autumn a hug.

When we entered the courtroom Shawn and I sat down together in the designated family section.

Shawn told me, "I'm tired of being pushed out." She looked beaten. She had to have felt terrible about missing Autumn's wedding, but she didn't say anything about that.

"For the past month, I have just wanted to hold Autumn and hug her, and tell her how much I love her," she said. Being a mother I could sympathize.

For most of the July trial, Judge Jones had sat holding her head up with one hand. A court artist had even drawn her doing so. She appeared only slightly more interested now that Autumn was there to be sentenced.

Autumn stood before the judge, facing her judgment day. She barely had two words out of her mouth when the tears started flowing.

"Your honor, I'm glad to have this opportunity to speak to the court," she started. "I know and appreciate the pain and embarrassment that this has caused Mr. Cosby. I wish he was here, and someday I hope to apologize in person."

Eight pages later, Autumn put down the hand written notes she had been reading from.

Fortunately, Judge Jones was lenient. It was the only positive move we had seen her make during the whole event. She had diverted from the federal guidelines, giving Autumn the choice of six months in the boot-type camp that Baum had originally told her about, or twenty-six months confinement in prison. Both options were much better than the dreaded five years she could have received. Yosie did receive a five year sentence and he was whisked away from the courtroom and back to jail.

When the proceedings were over, Shawn and I made our way to Autumn to hug her and walk out with her.

Autumn had to go to probation and sign some papers. She didn't want Shawn to come in with her, while she said it was okay if I did.

When we came out Shawn told Autumn, "Give me a call." However, I think she knew Autumn wouldn't call so she didn't even offer a phone number.

Jerold Jackson had shown up late for the sentencing and couldn't get into the courthouse. He was left outside standing in the crowd. We were told he was crying.

When we walked outside it was the worst it had ever been. More than a hundred reporters were surrounding us, and it was all we could do to stay standing. Shawn had maneuvered in front of Autumn trying to hold back the crowd. "Enough is enough!" she shouted.

Wendy, Autumn, and I jumped into a waiting car and locked the doors. Reporters were taking pictures through the windows.

"It's about time you face us," one of the reporters yelled. He was referring to the fact that we had entered the courthouse by the side door. Little did he know it was to avoid Shawn and not the press when Autumn used the unencumbered entrance.

Wendy told the driver to take us to the hotel where the interview with *Dateline* would be taking place. We were sent to a room where we had lunch, and regrouped while everything was made ready.

When we went to the room set up for shooting the interview, all the furniture had been removed except for two chairs—one for Ed Gordon, and one for Autumn. Surrounding them were equipment used for the taping, structures for the lighting, and several people for directing.

The adjoining room held the extra furniture, and a television had been tuned into the video cameras so that Baum, a few others, and I would be able to see and hear everything going on.

When Ed started his questions he threw Autumn by not asking his questions in context. Instead of asking her about the case, he asked her what she thought of her mother being referred to as a whore.

134

For several hours he asked her questions that she cautiously answered, being careful not to give away any unnecessary information.

When the questions where at last finished, we walked out of the room to see parts of the interview already being advertised on television.

Baum wanted Autumn to do a phone interview after that. Autumn was beyond exhausted. "It will have to wait," I told him.

When we were in the car to go back to our hotel, Wendy and I told Autumn how great she had done. But as great as she held up, she could have done a lot better. Ed had given her plenty of opportunities to get some real information out there.

When we returned to the hotel I asked her, "Why didn't you answer his questions like you said you wanted to do?"

"I just didn't want everyone knowing my personal business," she said.

"Why did you do the interview then?" I asked. "That was what this was supposed to be all about. People can't be sympathetic if you aren't open to them."

"You'll understand everything soon enough," she told me. "Let's leave it at that."

Chapter 19

FORTUNE COOKIES

"Autumn called," Richard said. "She has something to tell us."

We drove over to the lake house and knocked on Tony and Autumn's door.

"Sit down," Tony directed, after we had entered the lower story apartment Richard had put together for them under Lois's living area.

A kerosene heater was going, and it was cozy in the small living room.

"We have good news," Tony said. "In fact, we have two pieces of good news."

"Okay," Richard said, sounding ready to brace himself.

"Autumn's pregnant!"

I don't know if our mouths dropped open, but they could see we were not jumping for joy by any means.

"You told me you just had your period," I said to Autumn, puzzled.

"I didn't really have it," she confessed.

I remembered how when we were in New York she had mentioned her period every day, and how she carried on about having cramps and bloating.

"Why did you lie to me?" I asked her.

"I told her to," Tony said. "We wanted to tell you when we were ready."

"You've never been supportive of me getting pregnant," Autumn added.

"Not while you were facing prison," I told her.

Wanting to move past our disappointment, Tony tried to recapture some good cheer by announcing the second bit of good news. "Autumn won't have to go to prison now."

"What makes you think that?" Richard asked.

"Because she's pregnant. She can't do the exercises at the boot camp."

"No, now she'll have to go to prison for two years instead six months," I said. "And they'll take the baby away from her. Who is going to take care of it?"

"I am," said Tony.

Tony was due to be sentenced in a couple of weeks.

"What if you have to go to prison?" I asked.

"I won't," Tony said with smug confidence. "I talked to my lawyer and he's pretty sure I'm getting off."

"You're not responding the right way," Autumn said. She jumped up center stage. "You're always telling me I need to express myself, so I'm going to. Jewel doesn't love me unconditionally. I'm tired of everyone, Bill, my mother, Jewel, all thinking they can lord over me."

I had been the best aunt I could albeit too worrisome and a victim of raging PMS on occasion. Richard and Lois had done everything possible to help Autumn, and then some. We all had virtually put our lives on hold to see her through this.

"I'm not going to take this," I said.

"Sit down and be quiet," Richard said. He had continued to be a rock through the whole affair.

Tony jumped up and went in the kitchen, explosive words following behind him.

Richard followed, and in his usual way, tried to smooth things out.

"We have done everything we can to help you," I reminded Autumn.

"I never asked for your help!" she yelled back.

"And what would you have done if we hadn't helped you? You would still be sitting in jail."

"I would have figured something out."

It was pointless to argue. I walked out the door.

When Richard left to follow me Autumn stopped him and asked for $300.00 to pay her court fine.

"There's no one else to help her and she knows it," I told Richard when we were in the car.

I called Autumn a couple of days later, at Richard's encouragement, to talk to her about our fight. "You know Autumn, you talk about my unconditional love for you, but what about your unconditional love for me? I love you, but I don't think you love me."

She didn't have any response.

"This is the hardest thing any of us have had to go through, and your hormones are changing with the pregnancy. I told you I would stand by you until this is over, and I will keep to my word. I will come and visit you in prison like I said I would."

⸙

Every year during January, I pruned the rose bushes at Lois's house. She came out to help me, and told me Autumn received an extension from having to turn herself into prison until April.

When I saw Autumn and Tony I asked, "Why didn't you call and tell us about the extension?"

Tony's answer was, "You could have called us."

"How were we supposed to know to call you?" I asked. "We had an agreement that you were supposed to keep us informed."

Lois had handled the news of Autumn's pregnancy by running out and buying baby clothes. Then she paid for Autumn's and Tony's plane tickets to New York for Tony's sentencing.

Richard and I were called on to take them to the airport.

It came on the news that Tony had been excused from any sentence.

I couldn't believe it. Boris had received 3 months just for driving Autumn to the airport. Tony on the other hand was discharged with nothing more than probation. I wondered if it hadn't been for Tony's perfidy, if Autumn might have received a lighter sentence.

It was raining hard, and not showing any signs of letting up when Richard and I went to meet Autumn and Tony at the airport. They were to arrive at 11.00 p.m.

When the passengers were deplaning I had a small twinge of panic that they might not have made their flight, but then I saw them.

Autumn looked disheveled.

Once we were in the car Tony started talking about what had happened during his sentencing. "The judge really went on about everything," he said. "I was commended for coming forward right away, and for being so helpful with the case."

"Yeah," Autumn said under her breath. She was visibly disturbed about Tony getting off while she was pregnant and going to jail.

"It's too bad, Autumn didn't get off too," I said, my loyalties being for my niece. "We would really be celebrating then."

Changing the subject, Tony said, "I hate New York. When this is over I'm going to do a comedy on how stupid *Niggers* can be."

Shocked at his use of the "*N*" word, we covered our uneasiness with embarrassed giggles.

"This guy was sittin' five feet away from us saying 'its hur, its *hur!*'" Tony said, still visibly upset. He added that he had stared down more than one ogler and made faces at others.

In March Autumn called up and sweetly asked, "JJ, would you like to come to Newport Beach with Tony and me?"

I was flattered that she had asked. Things had been strained between us since the pregnancy announcement.

"Sure," I said eager for us to have the chance to make amends.

Tony had heard about a modeling search convention, and it was still his goal to be a model or an actor. He was sure he would get work from the audition. We made our plans to go.

Tony did a good job of performing during his video stint. Afterward, Autumn was wearing a proud smile. His success was hers. She had lived in the shadow of her mother, and now she was living in the shadow of Tony. You would have thought she was the one who had just done the performance. Unfortunately, no contracts for modeling or acting were forthcoming.

During a break, we went to lunch at a Chinese restaurant.

As usual, Autumn didn't have much to say with Tony present, so Tony and I carried on most of the conversation.

Autumn would laugh, acknowledge, giggle, and smile, but she conversed very little. Mostly, she rubbed her bulging belly, and was taken with what was happening inside of her body.

"Could you be having twins?" I asked her.

"I don't know," she said.

"You are so large. You either have your dates wrong, or it has to be twins."

When the fortune cookies came there were enough for two each. Autumn picked two fortunes exactly the same.

Tony and I looked at each other and in unison exclaimed, "Twins!"

Autumn sent out invitations for a baby shower. She tried to act like it was perfectly normal, that everything was always perfectly normal, but the big question was: What do you get a baby who is going to be born in prison?

Friends and family alike couldn't resist teasing about it.

"Black and white stripped pajamas," one friend said.

"How about a miniature ball and chain?" another chimed in.

"A tiny handcuff key," someone added.

The day after we returned from Newport Beach, Autumn called to say she had a sonogram and she was having twin boys.

"I couldn't be happier," Tony said. "I would have been just as happy if there had been four babies in her belly!"

Tony's delusion that Autumn wouldn't have to go to prison just because she was pregnant, was soon to be disproved. On April 22, 1998, just over one year and three months after the ordeal had started, Richard, Lois, Tony, and I delivered Autumn to prison.

FCI DUBLIN was a low security federal correctional institution with an adjacent minimum security satellite camp. It was located on an army base. Right across the street was a razor-wire fenced in prison for women doing hard time.

When we drove up, we came upon a grouping of wood-sided buildings painted beige. The barracks would be Autumn's new home until she could be admitted to a halfway house to finish out her pregnancy.

We pulled into a staff parking lot and a short-tempered guard told us she would take charge of Autumn, and that we had to leave immediately.

Some of the prisoners were hanging out the windows to watch Autumn's arrival.

Autumn and Tony shared a last kiss. His pink tongue prodded Autumn's mouth, and she gently kissed him back. Tears filled her eyes, and Tony tenderly wiped them away.

As Autumn waddled her way to her new destiny, I realized she would no longer be waking to the vision of the lake outside her front door, nor the warmth of her husband's arms. She was taking her two babies with her into an unknown future.

"Remember the butterflies!" I shouted to her. "Rise above this!"

"Yeah," Tony shouted. "Rise above this!"

A prisoner walked by and told us, "Don't worry, we'll take good care of her."

Once we were in the car, Tony burst into tears and cried the better part of the three-hour ride home.

"Autumn will charm the other inmates, and they will gather around her in support," I said.

"That's right," Lois said. "She can be very charming."

Autumn had been in prison less than a month when she was transferred to a halfway house in San Francisco.

On a sunny spring day in May we picked up Tony to go and see Autumn. We crossed the Golden Gate Bridge, drove through the city and

140

pulled up in front of the halfway facility on Taylor Street. It was in the Tenderloin District. It was an African American neighborhood, and the hotel across the street had signs painted on it advertising nude women. You could look at one for 25 cents, or talk to one for a dollar.

Autumn was waiting at the window of the unmarked apartment building.

Tony couldn't make his way to her fast enough.

Richard signed the papers to bring in Autumn's personal belongings. The guards looked like inmates themselves. They were wearing shorts and had most of their teeth missing.

Richard was holding a box and stepped onto the elevator to go to Autumn's room.

"Wait for me," I said.

Instead of being locked in their rooms, they were given keys to keep the other prisoners out. Autumn unlocked the room numbered 428.

Inside, it was long and narrow reminding me of a miniature boxcar. There was a single bed, with a single blanket. There was a built in place for a TV, and a plastic shelf above the bed for clothes. A tiny bathroom was off to the side. She had spent two days without any provisions inside of what reminded me of a nun's cubby.

On the way down a black male prisoner asked, "When's the boy coming?"

"Boys!" Autumn corrected, rubbing her enormous belly.

Chapter 20

BUTTERFLY TRANSFORMATIONS

There is nothing like a baby, except maybe two babies, to heal the wounds in a family. Lois and I went to see Autumn's babies for the first time since they had been born. We were laden with a bushel of gifts.

Autumn was allowed to stay at the halfway house for three months with her babies before they would be taken away from her and given to Tony.

When she came out of the elevator, she was wheeling a baby carriage covered with receiving blankets.

Her hair was slicked back and she had makeup on. Motherhood had agreed with her and given her an edge of maturity that she was previously lacking.

Autumn woke the babies up so that we could play with them. When she went to change Trevor's diaper he peed on her, not once, but twice.

She laughed and delighted in the miracle of her son.

"Look at what Trey does," she said, holding him up and kissing him on the lips. "He makes the funniest face when I do that."

I was glad to see she had taken to being a devoted mother and that she was very comfortable in her new role.

"Can we take some pictures?" Lois asked.

"Oh no," said Autumn. "The guards don't allow it."

The guards weren't around, and I was pretty sure it was just an excuse. Ever since Autumn's arrest she hadn't let anyone take pictures if she could help it. She didn't have any control over all the pictures the press had taken, so she made every effort to control the pictures that were taken by the family.

After opening her gifts, she asked us not to buy her anything else. She just wanted gift certificates that she could use at K-Mart. "The mothers get to go shopping at K-Mart on Mondays to get their diapers and stuff," she told us.

As Lois and I oo'ed and ah'ed over her babies, Autumn told us she hadn't let anyone else hold them. "I keep them covered up whenever I leave my room."

The twins were going to be much darker skinned than Autumn, at least they were so far. Like all babies, they were as cute and precious as could be. They didn't turn out to be identical twins, and their personalities were as different as their looks.

"Baum is working on an appeal," Autumn told us during the visit. "I don't want to have to go back to the prison."

Appeals take a long time so she did have to go back to the Dublin prison for the time being. Lois helped Tony bring the babies home.

Tony hadn't been taking care of them long when he told me, "I've never had so much respect for how much mothers do."

He said this while sitting between the twins, who were propped up in their highchairs, alternately feeding them tiny spoonfuls of baby food.

Tony would take the twins down to be with Autumn most weekends, and I went down every three or four weeks. I would send her letters and more bedtime stories to read in between.

Autumn and Tony hadn't allowed Shawn to see the babies at first, but then they relented. When Shawn came up to see the babies she had bought Autumn's sisters along.

I went over to Lois's to see my sister-in-law and other nieces. I was surprised when I saw Shawn. In New York, she had looked great with her voluptuous breasts, and short sassy haircut. However, in the past year she had grown quite heavy and wasn't put together like she had been in New York City. Then again, I wasn't either. I had gone back to my quiet country life and let my hair grow out too. I had packed my New York suits, stylish shoes, and winter coat—tucking them away indefinitely.

I went down to visit Autumn mid-April, 1999.

"I wasn't expecting you until tomorrow," she said. I could tell that I had caught her off guard. Her hair was brushed straight back, and it was growing long, hanging down enough to cover her long thin neck.

I had nearly forgotten how she talked with her hands.

"How come Tony isn't coming down this weekend?" I asked.

"He's building the boys a sandbox."

She always jumped to his defense. The man didn't work so he could build a sandbox anytime.

"He should be here every weekend."

"Most of the women in here have lost their men within the first six months," she said. "Tony comes as much as he can. My first year will be up April 22nd," she said, trying to change the subject.

Maybe you were smart to get pregnant. It has kept Tony around," I said, giving her an all-knowing smile.

She smiled back and tilted her head in a discerning fashion.

As we continued our visit, I told Autumn, "Your mother has really gained a lot of weight."

"She's been that heavy before. I'd rather see her heavy than doing drugs."

"That's for sure," I agreed. Shawn did appear to be doing well, and I was glad for that.

"I wrote my mother and told her she has to take care of her own children now," Autumn said. "I have my own family to take care of. I love my brother and sisters like they were my own, but they're not. They're my mother's responsibility." She pressed her petite hands flat on the top of the small round table where we were sitting.

"I'm so glad Lois has been able to help take care of the kids for you. I didn't have it in me to do it. The part I like best about your children is that I can enjoy them and then give them back. Lois is a real champ. Trevor is getting so heavy I don't know how she picks him up."

"I know," Autumn said, beaming with pride. "He weighs 27 pounds!"

Trey was the smaller of the two boys.

It was only two months until the twins would have their first birthday.

"You must miss them when Tony doesn't bring them down for the weekend."

"I do." Sadness glazed her eyes. "I might get to go on a furlough soon," she added cheerfully.

"In that case, you'd better head to the closest hotel with Tony!"

"That's for sure!" she said grinning.

"That must be the hardest part of being in prison; not being able to have conjugal visits."

"If we did, everyone would be pregnant," she said rudimentarily.

Autumn always had pragmatic answers to give. She enjoyed problem solving, and was able to rise above her emotional needs. However, growing up in a dysfunctional household didn't give her much opportunity to be heard and her lack of communication skills had been a drawback. At last, she was coming out of that shell and finding her voice.

We went outside where she could smoke and we could enjoy the fresh spring air.

"I know I caused Cosby and his family a lot of grief. I know how hard this has been on you and Uncle Ricky and grandma," Autumn confessed.

Autumn had spent a lot of time thinking about what had transpired, and I was glad that she was having some heartfelt realizations. For several hours we talked about the lessons she had learned, and the things she wanted to change about her life.

"All I want to do is be home with my babies. I want to put this all behind me."

"Do you think you'll ever get the blood test done to see if Cosby is your dad or not?"

"No, and I don't care one way or the other. I just want to move forward. I just want to be a family and be with my family."

❧⋯⋯⋯⋯

Baum did win Autumn an appeal. She was taken out a back gate of the prison to avoid the press that had collected out in front. She was home just in time for her babies' birthday party, like she hoped she would be.

However, her joy would be short lived. The prosecution pushed to have the appeal overturned because of a negative ruling in a similar case.

Though Baum pointed out the differences in Autumn's case, the appeal was still overturned, and after a few months reprieve she was sent back to the half-way house to finish out her sentence.

One afternoon, before she went back to prison, Richard and I, Lois, Tony, Autumn, and the babies were all hanging out in Lois's living room.

Richard and I were arguing with Tony and Autumn about the division of the proceeds from a possible book sale—one that eventually fell through.

Lois grew bored with the bickering and passionately exclaimed, "What if it turns out Cosby isn't your father? Then what? There isn't going to be any book!"

Silence filled the room as we each tried to comprehend what we had just heard. Lois had held to the fact that Autumn was Cosby's child for twenty-two years and all through the trial. Did she know something she had withheld all this time?

"What are you saying?" I asked.

"Nothing. Really . . . I'm just tired of this whole mess. I want it to go away. I'm tired of all the fighting and arguments. There are the boys to think of now." It wasn't long after that outburst that Lois was on television pleading with Cosby to recognize his first grandchildren—the twins.

Autumn had to be affected by her grandmother's first ever words of uncertainty even though they had been quickly recanted. In her heart, she would always be Cosby's "love child" no matter if a blood test revealed otherwise. She had lived her life believing it, and until now had no reason not to. Her firm belief was that the voice behind Fat Albert, belonged to her father.

Princess Autumn's castle made of television air-waves had crumbled beneath her. The comedian dad she was waiting to rescue her had wavered out of focus.

Autumn's sense of who she was had been caught in a rouse that Cosby had helped to perpetuate. Whether she was of his blood or not, he had given her cause to think she was. You don't support someone for twenty-two years without motivation.

As far as a paternity test, Autumn and Cosby had remained on opposite ends of the pole. First Autumn wanted one and Cosby refused, then Cosby said he would take one and she refused at the recommendation of her attorney. Again, she decided maybe it would be best and he refused, possibly at the council of his attorney. Ultimately, it was never done.

Autumn never doubted for one second that Cosby was her father. Her mother and grandmother had been telling her as much since she was of the age of memory. She has never had reason to think otherwise. If you think about it, there are probably a lot of bastard children running about the Hollywood hills—all with celebrity parents. It wasn't that much of a stretch to think that she was one of them.

※

Autumn finally finished her prison sentence, but not before Tony had left her. He had left the children with Lois. Two years had turned out to be a year too long.

After Autumn was released she moved with Lois to Los Angeles where they rented a house with Shawn and her girls. Lois took care of the twins while Shawn and Autumn worked.

Autumn had grown leaps and bounds, and was no longer the teenager she appeared to be when she was twenty-two.

She had moved forward. She had two young boys to raise, and that would be an honorable challenge.

As life goes, there will be other tribulations for Autumn to face. But there is one thing I am certain of, genetic or otherwise, she inherited a celebrity's sense of wit and charisma. She will continue to charm and enamor everyone she meets along her way.

BIBLIOGRAPHY

01/17/97	Sharon Waxman, *Cosby's Son Shot to Death Near L.A. Freeway,* Special to The Washington Post
01/20/97	Writer Unknown, Report: *Two Arrested in Cosby Extortion Plot,* Washington (Reuter)
01/20/97	Writer Unknown, *Cosby subject of extortion attempt,* New York, (UPI)
01/21/97	Writer Unknown, *2 Are Arrested in Plot Against Bill Cosby, Extortion Case Appears Unrelated to Son's Death,* The Washington Post
01/21/97	Writer Unknown, *Potential Witnesses Questioned in Cosby Murder,* Los Angeles (Reuter)
01/22/97	Howard Kurtz, Washington Post Staff Writer, *A Pawn in Her Game? The Globe & Cosby's Alleged Extortionist,* The Washington Post
01/22/97	Writer Unknown, *Cosby extortion suspects in court,* New York, (UPI)
01/22/97	Writer Unknown, *Cosby extortion suspects hit CBS, too,* New York (UPI)
01/24/97	Michelle DeArmond, Associated Press Writer, *Cosby Extortionist's 'Dad' Speaks,* Los Angeles (AP)
01/24/97	Samuel Maull, Associated Press Writer, *Cosby Extort Suspects' Bail Set,* New York (AP)
01/25/97	Al Guart in New York, David K. Ll in Los Angeles, *Trucker says he's Cos suspects real father,* New York Post
01/25/97	Michele Salcedo, Staff Writer, *Judge Sets Bond in Extort Case,* Newsday
01/25/97	J. Zamgba Browne, Amsterdam News Staff, *FBI nabs woman trying to extort $40 million from Cosby,* New York Amsterdam News
01/27/97	Verena Dobnik, Associated Press Writer, Verena Dobnik, *Bill Cosby Returns to Work,* New York (AP)
01/27/97	Verena Dobnik, Associated Press Writer, Verena Dobnik, *Cosby Admits to Affair,* New York (AP)

01/27/97	Writer Unknown, *Cosby says he had 'rendezvous' with Autumn Jackson's mother,* New York (AP)
01/28/97	Andrea Peyser, *Why we're willing to forgive Perfect Family Man,* New York Post
01/28/97	Writer Unknown, *Cosby's Wife Says Affair Is No Longer An Issue,* Los Angeles (Reuter)
01/28/97	Michele Saledo, Staff Writer, *Extortion Suspect Out on Bail,* Newsday
01/28/97	Writer Unknown, *Boyfriend of Alleged Cosby Extortionist Pleads,* New York (Reuter)
01/28/97	Gail Appleson, Law Correspondent, *UPDATE: Boyfriend of Accused Cosby Extortionist Pleads Guilty,* New York (Reuter)
01/28/97	John J. Goldman, Jane Hall, Times Staff Writers, *Anguished Cosby: 'I Want to Talk',* Los Angeles Times Report on Ennis Cosby Murder
01/28/97	Al Guart, Cathy Burke, *COSBY SPEAKS OUT: TRYSTS WITH HER MOM But denies he's woman's dad,* New York Post
01/29/97	Greg B. Smith, Daily News, Staff Writer, *COSBY EXTORT CASE: Suspect makes a deal,* Daily News
01/29/97	Lynette Holloway, *Man Pleads Guilty to Charges Tided to Cosby Extortion Plot,* The New York Times METRO
01/29/97	Howard Rosenberg, Times Television Critic, *For Cosby Coverage, It's Business as Usual,* Los Angeles Times
01/29/97	Inquirer Wire Service, *Guilty plea set in Cosby extortion plot,* Philadelphia Inquirer, National
01/29/97	Al Guart, Cathy Burke, *Cosby **'love child'** beau pleads guilty in extort plot,* New York Post
01/30/97	Gerald Easley, Democrat Staff Writer, *Cosby, extortion and a Tallahassee tie,* Tallahassee Democrat
01/30/97	Michele Salcedo, Staff Writer, *A Legacy of Deceit, Extortion suspect guilty in '90 fraud,* Newsday
01/31/97	Lawrie Mifflin, *CBS Says It Would Be Unseemly To Broadcast Cosby Interview,* The New York Times
01/31/97	Al Guart, Cathy Burke, *Con man eyed as mastermind of Cosby plot,* New York Post
01/31/97	Michele Salcedo, Staff Writer, *Kansas: Keep Him in Jail,* Newsday

01/31/97	Greg B. Smith, Jere Hester, Daily News Staff Writers, *Cos suspect: I was duped,* Daily News
01/31/97	Writer Unknown, *Cosby plot suspect: I didn't want $40M,* United Press International
02/13/97	Gail Appleson, Law Correspondent, *Woman Indicted in Cosby Extortion Case,* New York (Reuter)
02/20/97	Gail Appleson, Law Correspondent, *UPDATE: Woman Pleads Not Guilty In Cosby Extortion Case,* New York (Reuter)
02/20/97	Writer Unknown, *Lawyer: Evidence will prove woman is Cosby's daughter,* New York (AP)
02/20/97	Larry Neumeister, Associated Press Writer, *Cosby 'Daughter' Pleads Innocent,* New York (AP)
02/21/97	Larry Neumeister Associated Press Writer, *Woman Insists Cosby is her dad,* New York (AP)
02/24/97	Writer Unknown, Web posted, *Judge orders lawyers not to discuss evidence in Cosby case,* New York (AP)
02/28/97	Larry Neumeister, Associated Press Writer, *4th Held in Cosby Extortion Plot,* New York (AP)
04/10/97	Writer Unknown, *Mother Walks Off Geraldo Show In Cosby Case,* New York (Reuter)
06/27/97	Writer Unknown, *Cosby to Testify at Extortion Trial,* New York (AP)
07/01/97	Greg B. Smith, *Blood test? No kin do, says Cosby,* Daily News
07/08/97	Tom Hays, *Defendant's mother speaks about Cosby extortion case,* New York (AP)
07/08/97	Benjamin Weiser, *A woman takes a lie detector test to rebut charges of extorting money from a star.,* The New York Times
07/09/97	Gail Appleson, *Cosby's Image Targeted,* New York (AP)
07/10/97	Larry Neumeister, *Woman Wonders if Cosby Hid Her Because She's 'His Half-White Daughter',* New York (AP)
07/10/97	Benjamin Weiser, *Questions in Cosby Case: Scheme or Plea for Help?,* The New York Times
07/11/97	Bob Herbert, *No Mercy for Autumn,* The Press Democrat, Santa Rosa, CA

07/13/97	Denise-Marie Santiago, Inquirer Staff Writer, *Plot thickens in Cosby extortion trial,* Philadelphia Inquirer-National
07/13/97	Bob Herbert, *And if she is Cosby's daughter?,* The Press Democrat, Santa Rosa, CA
07/14/97	Writer Unknown, *Attorney for Bill Cosby Takes the Stand,* New York 1 News
07/14/97	Tom Hays, *Yosi Medina May Have Been Involved in Cosby Plot, Extortionist or Mystic,* New York (AP)
07/15/97	Writer Unknown, *Cosby says he bought silence after affair,* New York (CNN)
07/15/97	Writer Unknown, *Cosby takes stand in extortion trial,* New York (CNN)
07/15/97	Tom Hays, *Bill Cosby's Testimony Looms At Woman's Extortion Trial,* New York (AP)
07/15/97	Tom Hays, Cosby: *'I am Not Your Father',* New York (AP)
07/16/97	Larry Neumeister, *Cosby Called Deadbeat Dad,* New York (AP)
07/17/97	Tom Hays, *Cosby Defendant Describes Bitter 'Kodak Moment',* New York (AP)
07/18/97	Tom Hays, *Jackson Swore That Cosby Was Her Father,* New York (AP)
07/21/97	Tom Hays, *Cosby Prosecution Rests,* New York (AP)
07/21/97	Jill Smolowe, *Autumn of His Life?,* Time Magazine
07/22/97	Gail Appleson, *Grandmom: Cosby's the dad, Claims she filled in Autumn, I told her to keep quiet,* The Philadelphia Daily News
07/22/97	Eric Stirgus, Rita Delfiner, *Video 'bears' Cosby's tender first meeting with Autumn,* New York Post
07/22/97	Tom Hays, *Cosby Jury Breaks for Day,* New York (AP)
07/22/97	Writer Unknown, *Both sides rest in Cosby extortion trial,* New York (Reuter)
07/22/97	Benjamin Weiser, *Jury Sees Tape of Defendant With Cosby,* The New York Times
07/22/97	Graham Rayman, *Granny: Cos Sent $14,000,* Newsday
07/22/97	Andrea Peyser, *Advice he never gave her: Get a lawyer!,* New York Post
07/23/97	Benjamin Weiser, *The Cosby Case Nears a Close With a Dispute Over Which One Is the Real Victim,* The New York Times

07/24/97	Tom Hays, *Cosby extortion case is in the hands of the jury,* New York (AP)
07/25/97	Writer Unknown, *Autumn Jackson convicted of extortion,* New York (AP)
07/25/97	Joal Ryan, *Guilty Verdict in Cosby Extortion Plot,* E! Online News
07/25/97	Jan M. Faust, *Jackson Guilty in Cosby Trial,* ABCNEWS.com
07/25/97	Sarah Drain, *Jurors say Jackson misled,* New York (UPI)
07/25/97	Writer Unknown, *Jurors felt woman intended to ruin Cosby's reputation,* New York (CNN)
07/26/97	Eric Stirgus, Ann V. Bollinger & Rita Delfiner, **'LOVE CHILD'** *BEGS FOR BILL'S HELP,* New York Post
07/26/97	Andrea Peyser, *Take the Paternity test Bill, and quit being a hypocrite,* New York Post
07/26/97	Maggie Haberman, *Neighbors want star to show mercy,* New York Post
07/26/97	Greg B. Smith, *TAKE A BIG FALL She's convicted of Cosby extort: Dad image in doghouse?,* Daily News
07/26/97	Linda Deutsch, AP Special Correspondent, *Juries May Be Star Struck,* Los Angeles (AP)
07/26/97	Catherine Crocker, Associated Press Writer, *Cosby Juror: Jury Felt Sorry for Defendant,* New York (AP)
07/28/97	Writer Unknown, *Bill Cosby Gives Blood For Paternity Test - Lawyer,* Los Angeles (Reuter)
07/29/97	Writer Unknown, *Woman refuses to see if Bill Cosby is her father,* New York (CNN)
07/29/97	Richard Cohen, *Bill Cosby's Best Pitch,* The Washington Post
07/29/97	Andy Soltis, *Cosby on* **love-child** *paternity: I'LL TAKE BLOOD TEST,* New York Post
07/31/97	Writer Unknown, *Lawyer: Autumn may submit to blood test,* New York (UPI)
08/01/97	Writer Unknown, *Bill Cosby at Konocti Harbor Resort,* Lifestyle TODAY! Magazine
08/05/97	Writer Unknown, *Why Cosby* **'love child'** *was hog-tied in court,* National Enquirer

08/12/97	Writer Unknown, *Please, Bill, Don't let our baby go to jail...*, Globe
11/06/97	Al Guart, *Autumn weds her turncoat accomplice,* New York Post
12/08/97	Andrea Peyser, *AUTUMN'S APPEAL FOR MERCY IS A LOST COS,* New York Post
12/10/97	Al Guart, *AUTUMN'S 'DAD' INSISTS HE WASN'T PAID TO PLAY PAPA,* New York Post
12/11/97	Al Guart, *Cosby prosecutors fear wrist-slap for Autumn,* New York Post
12/11/97	Gail Appleson, Law Correspondent, *Woman To Be Sentenced In Cosby Extortion Case,* New York (Reuters)
12/12/97	Writer Unknown, *Autumn Jackson Sentenced to 26 Months,* ABCNEWS.com
12/12/97	Gail Appleson, Las Correspondent, *U.S. woman gets prison term in Cosby extortion scheme,* New York (Reuters)
12/12/97	Writer Unknown, *Jackson weeps during sentencing for Cosby plot,* New York (CNN)
12/13/97	Greg B. Smith, *Autumn's fall is capped with 26-month sentence, She apologizes to Cosby as judge urges boot camp,* Daily News
12/13/97	Michele McPhee, *Three jurors weigh in on jail time,* Daily News
12/13/97	Andrea Peyser, *Confused kid does time while 'killers' walk,* New York Post
12/13/97	Benjamin Weiser, *Autumn Jackson Receives 26-Month Term in Cosby Case,* The New York Times
12/14/97	Writer Unknown, *Autumn stunned that Cos turned her in,* New York (UPI)
12/15/97	Andrea Peyser, *WORST FOR AUTUMN IS LOSING HER ONLY 'DAD',* New York Post
12/16/97	Writer Unknown, *COSBY'S SECRET PAYOFF TO LOVE CHILD'S DAD,* Globe
12/17/97	Writer Unknown, *Cosby Talks About Autumn Jackson,* New York (AP)
12/17/97	Larry Neumeister, Associated Press Writer, *Man Sentenced in Cosby Money Plot,* New York (AP)
12/17/97	Writer Unknown, *Man who aided Cosby plot gets 3-month sentence,* New York (Reuters)

12/20/97	Al Guart, *PREGNANT AUTUMN IS FACING BOOTY CAMP,* New York Post
12/20/97	Writer Unknown, *Autumn Jackson cites pregnancy in appeal,* New York (AP)
01/23/98	Gail Appleson, Law Correspondent, *Defendant in Cosby Scheme Gets Probation,* New York (Reuters)
04/20/98	Andrea Peyser, *AUTUMN HAS COS TO REGRET,* New York Post
07/09/98	Writer Unknown, *Twins born to extortionist,* The Sacramento Bee
06/09/99	Writer Unknown, *Extortion Conviction in Cosby Case Thrown Out,* New York (Reuters)
06/10/99	Writer Unknown, *Woman in Cosby extortion case released from prison,* Dublin, CA (CNN)
11/16/99	Benjamin Weiser, *Judges Reinstate Conviction In Extortion of Bill Cosby,* The New York Times

Be sure to pick up a copy of the short stories that were read to Autumn during her ordeal:

TUMBLEWEED: And Other Adult Bedtime Stories

To learn more about the author, you are invited to visit the website of Jewel Star. (Her books are available for purchase on her site.):

http://www.JewelStarAuthor.com

For access to a complete list of books by Jewel Star please visit:

http://www.amazon.com/author/jewelstar

To Contact the author directly:

JewelStarAuthor@gmail.com

Your review is very important, not only to provide important feedback for the author, but to future readers. Please take a moment to leave your positive thoughts on Star's Amazon's Author's Page. You opinion is greatly appreciated.

www.amazon.com/author/jewelstar